Creepy Colleges
and Haunted Universities
True Ghost Stories

Cynthia Thuma & Catherine Lower

Schiffer
Publishing Ltd

4880 Lower Valley Road, Atglen, PA 19310 USA

Dedications

To our husbands, David and Jim, and our children,
Kirstie and Nick, for putting up with their absentee moms.

Designed by John P. Cheek
Cover design by Bruce Waters
Type set in Casablanca Antique/Korinna BT

ISBN: 0-7643-1805-5
Printed in China

Published by Schiffer Publishing Ltd.
4880 Lower Valley Road
Atglen, PA 19310
Phone: (610) 593-1777; Fax: (610) 593-2002
E-mail: Info@schifferbooks.com
Please visit our web site catalog at **www.schifferbooks.com**
We are always looking for people to write books on new and related subjects.
If you have an idea for a book, please contact us at the above address.

This book may be purchased from the publisher.
Include $3.95 for shipping.
Please try your bookstore first.
You may write for a free catalog.

In Europe, Schiffer books are distributed by
Bushwood Books
6 Marksbury Avenue
Kew Gardens
Surrey TW9 4JF England
Phone: 44 (0) 20 8392 8585
Fax: 44 (0) 20 8392 9876
E-mail: Bushwd@aol.com
Free postage in the UK. Europe: air mail at cost.

Special Thanks

Writing a book of this sort requires the help of many and we have been fortunate to find a plethora of kind souls who have been generous and helpful to the max. They provided background material, served as direct sources of information, and connected us with other experts on their campuses...and sometimes even provided leads to other haunted campuses. We are grateful for their generous assistance and encouragement.

Alabama: Patsy Sears, reference librarian, University of Montevallo, Montevallo

Arkansas: Dr. Brooks Blevins, director of regional studies, Mabee-Simpson Library, Lyon College, Batesville

Frances McLean, Class of 1946, Henderson State University, Arkadelphia

California: Marie Felde, director, Office of Public Affairs, and Paul Parish, Faculty Club bartender, University of California, Berkeley

Delaware: Ed Okonowicz, editor, University Relations, University of Delaware, Newark

Florida: Anonymous source, Florida Atlantic University, Boca Raton

Laurin Bosse, director, College Relations, Flagler College, St. Augustine

Dr. Carolyn Bloomer and Rosie Folz, Ringling School of Art and Design, Sarasota

Rick Leffel, Delray Beach

Tracy Porter, Broward Community College, Class of 1991

Dania Rivero, Nova Southeastern University, Class of 1994

Brooks Terry, lifestyle editor, *FSView and Florida Flambeau*, Florida State University, Tallahassee

Georgia: Chris Duke, staff writer, *The Campus Carrier*, Berry College, Mount Berry

Hawai'i: Ku'ulei Pau, residential life coordinator, Student Housing Services, University of Hawai'i at Manoa, Honolulu

Idaho: Kathleen Craven, public relations officer, Boise State University, Boise

Illinois: Vicki Woodard, spokesperson, Eastern Illinois University, Charleston

Iowa: Dr. James Phifer, president, and Amy Johnson, director of public relations, Coe College, Cedar Rapids

Rod Library reference staff, University of Northern Iowa, Cedar Falls

Katherine Svec, Iowa State University Memorial Union marketing coordinator, Ames

Indiana: Rev. Robert A. Austgen, retired chaplain, University of Notre Dame health services, South Bend

Kansas: Linda Glasgow, librarian/archivist, Riley County Historical Museum, Manhattan

Cindy Von Ellig, archivist, Kansas State University, Manhattan

Dana Slaughter Rati, Kansas State University, Class of 1997

Kentucky: Lynn Niedermeier, archival assistant, Western Kentucky University, Bowling Green

Maryland: Nancy Gonce, university archivist, Towson University, Towson.

Massachusetts: Sara K. Streett, archives assistant, Smith College, Northampton

Nicole B. Tourangeau, CRM, college archivist and special collections librarian, Stonehill College, Easton

Michigan: Rita Abent, executive director of marketing and communications; Dr. David Woike, professor and interim music department head and Mary Ida Yost, retired professor and organist, Eastern Michigan University, Ypsilanti.

David Lower, production manager, Olympia Entertainment and the Fox Theatre, Detroit

Russell Magnaghi, university historian, and William M. McKinney, custodian, Plant Operations, Northern Michigan University, Marquette

Central Michigan University Public Relations and Marketing Office, Mount Pleasant

Minnesota: Jeff Sauve, assistant archivist, Rolvaag Memorial Library, St. Olaf College, Northfield.

Mississippi: Dr. Chester McKee, professor of electrical engineering and vice president emeritus, Mississippi State University, Starkville

Missouri: Dr. Alan Havig, professor of history, Stephens College, Columbia

Montana: Ashley Oliverio, public relations coordinator, Carroll College, Helena

Rita Munzenrider, director, University Relations, University of Montana, Missoula

Nebraska: Jessica Kennedy, marketing manager, Sheldon Memorial Art Gallery, University of Nebraska, Lincoln

New Hampshire: Michael Matros, director of college relations, Keene State College, Keene

New York: Betty Allen, special collections librarian, Schaeffer Library, Union College, Schenectady

Wendy Anthony, special collections associate, Skidmore College, Saratoga Springs

Helen T. Bergamo, curatorial archivist, Louis Jefferson Long Library, Wells College, Aurora.

North Carolina: Amy Guthrie, research assistant, Wilson Library, University of North Carolina, Chapel Hill

Georgia Williams, reference assistant, Chowan College, Murfreesboro

Ohio: Tamar Chute, associate university archivist, and Liz Cook, editor, University Relations, Ohio State University, Columbus

Carol Marshall, reading room coordinator, Olin & Chalmer Libraries, Kenyon College, Gambier

Susan Rouault, assistant director, College Relations, Baldwin-Wallace College, Berea

Dorrie Wells, operations administrator, School of Physical Activity and Educational Services, Ohio State University, Columbus

Oregon: Jeff Grundon, assistant director of athletics and admissions, Pacific University, Forest Grove

Pennsylvania: Allen Campbell, author, *Ghosts at Carlisle Barracks Army War College*, Carlisle

Jean Dolan, assistant director of college relations; Douglas Rosentrater, professor of communications, and Sandra Sobek-Allen, security guard, Bucks County Community College, Newtown

Eileen Zolotorofe, special projects coordinator, Bucks County Community College Foundation, Newtown

Dr. David Gnage, chief executive officer, Penn State University, Mont Alto Campus, Mont Alto

Christine Murphy, director of college relations, Muhlenberg College,Allentown

Mary Dolheimer, director of media relations, Gettysburg College, Gettysburg

Shannon Rosentrater, University of Pittsburgh, Class of 2006

Rhode Island: Kristine Hendrickson, director of communications, Salve Regina University, Newport

Texas: Judy Larson, head of public services, Sueltenfuss Library, Our Lady of the Lake University, San Antonio

Dr. Mairi C. Rennie, director, Armstrong Browning Library, Baylor University, Waco

Utah: Patrick William, senior writer, Public Relations and Marketing;

Colin Johnson, head, Theatre Arts Department, Utah State University, Logan

Virginia: Dr. Rita Mae Brown, Afton

Sherry McDonald, College of William and Mary, Class of 2000

Ann Romer, Richmond

Judy Watkins, Virginia Tourism Corporation, Richmond

Wisconsin: Michele M. Reid, director of libraries, Ripon College, Ripon

Wyoming: Diane Martin, library assistant, John Taggart Hinckley Library, and Laurel Vredenburg, director of publications, Northwest College, Powell.

Introduction

College ghost stories are a bit like college mascots – every school has at least one and they are generally entertaining. College ghost stories and tales of haunted buildings on campus tend to age, though whether it's like a fine wine or a ripe cheese, is up to the interpretation of the reader. Over the years they tend to take on something of a patina, a softer image and a bit of embellishment and as a result, they add to campus life and folklore. They mightily impress gullible freshmen.

Novelist and screenwriter Rita Mae Brown likes to break human experience into three categories: Subrational – the level of experience of plants and animals of lower intelligence; rational – the level of experience that is measurable or quantifiable; and superrational.

In the superrational realm, "it's silent, but things are happening," she told an audience of journalists a few years back. "Most of us have had these experiences, but conventional wisdom has told us to shut up about them."

While many of the tales here are set up at the rational level, we hope our readers will experience them through their superrational filter.

College is a bold step for young adults, a time of independence fraught with concern, a time of rapid intellectual and emotional growth, a time of uncertainty in an environment of order and rationality. Students are away from the guidance and daily counsel of their parents, many for the first sustained time. They're testing their wings in a grown-up world and hoping they're not looking too awkward doing so.

Freshmen first learn their college's ghost stories and other legends at orientation or through the dormitory staff. Some schools with extensive haunted histories offer freshman ghost tours.

Over the years, the dorm, building, or theater ghost becomes a familiar part of college life and lore, an old companion. Of all the stories in this book, there are no tales of vengeful, hurtful, or destructive ghosts. That fact is not accomplished through design. Some are reported to be sad, miffed, disappointed or aloof, but the majority are portrayed from benign to playful, helpful, kind-hearted, and even nurturing and motherly. We tried, but could not find reports of one vile, wrathful apparition. They simply aren't out there.

While ghost stories in general mirror the mores and social customs of their eras, the attributes of the ghosts seem to reflect how students and college faculty and employees view their lives on campus – of caring, learning, helping, and expanding one's realm of possibilities. The college experience exposes students to critical thinking and to challenging ideas and expanding them. Ghost stories, legends, and folklore make the college experience a bit richer, help put campus life in context, encourage students to open their minds, and dwell – if just for a moment – within the superrational.

Alabama

Huntingdon College

Two things were undeniably apparent from the day Martha set foot on Huntingdon's campus – she loved the color red and she was seriously depressed.

A New Yorker, Martha was in Montgomery more as a matter of duty than preference. The terms of her father's will directed that she attend her mother and grandmother's alma mater before she could benefit from his considerable estate.

She wore a red dress onto the campus and as she unpacked her luggage in Pratt Hall, where she was to live on the fourth floor, nearly everything she pulled out was red. The drapery, linens, right down to her fingernail lacquer, her Turkish prayer rug and the bric-a-brac she placed on her shelves were all red.

It's probably a natural conclusion that anyone so attached to the vivid, splashy color would have a personality to match, but Martha did not. She was shy and withdrawn on her good days, cold and sullen on the others.

Her first roommate could not stand Martha's dour, toxic personality and requested to move to another room. Her second roommate didn't last long, either. Still others came…and left. Finally, the dormitory's president, a kind-hearted, gregarious young woman, moved in, determined to win Martha over.

She, too, failed.

Martha spotted the dispirited woman as she packed her belongings and began a tirade, vilifying her and the other women in the dorm. She ended her rant with an ominous promise, one that troubled the dorm president: *Leave me and this room and you'll regret it forever.*

After the dorm president's departure, Martha's behavior became more bizarre and her depression spiraled deeper and deeper into darkness. At nights, unable to sleep, she wandered the halls of Pratt and other buildings. Only after hours and hours of aimless walking would she return to her room, curl up under her red blanket and fall deeply asleep.

One evening after Martha failed to leave her room, the dorm president went up to the fourth floor to talk to her. The door was open and all the red within glowed. She peeked into the room and screamed. The women downstairs heard a loud but dull thud and raced up the stairway, not knowing what to expect.

On the fourth floor hallway lay the dorm president, unconscious. A few feet away, draped across the bed was Martha, dead of self-inflicted slashes to her wrists. The blood that had flowed from her body was the same color as her bedclothes and the bedspread that covered her.

Martha still goes for her long, aimless walks in Pratt Hall and she is sometimes spotted looking wistfully out the hall's front window at night. Each year, on the anniversary of her suicide, students look for crimson light in the transom over her fourth-floor window, which now is a sorority chapter room.

The campus's other ghost also has a colorful name. He's the Ghost on the Green, because he ended his life on the campus green and now walks it at night. Students have felt him brush by or bump into them, but when they turn to see who it is, no one is there.

Auburn University

Every theater crackles with energy just before the curtain rises, and particularly so on premiere night. At Auburn University, the Telfair Peet Theatre radiates with a different sort of energy at the start of a production.

Sydney Grimlett, a Confederate soldier whose spirit once resided in University Chapel, apparently became a theater buff in the 1970s and moved to Telfair Peet after its opening in 1972. He shows up to watch when a play goes into production and often lingers on through opening night.

Sydney suffered severe injuries in the Civil War and was brought to Auburn, where the chapel and Old Main building had been pressed into service as hospitals. His injuries necessitated the amputation of a leg. In those days, before antibiotics, antiseptics, and sulfa drugs, amputations were a last resort and amputees, Sydney included, often died as a result of the procedure.

Sydney is known to rattle lockers, doors, machinery and other objects for no apparent reason. When he's visiting, drawers fly open, lights go on and off backstage and props and other stage equipment disappear.

During rehearsals and performances, he has been heard strolling the catwalks overhead and in the dressing room hallways. To help appease Sydney and keep him quiet, theater students leave a snack of M&Ms on one of the catwalks.

University of Montevallo

Many dorms today allow microwaves in student rooms, but in past years, every dorm had a resident or two who broke the rules by bringing in a hot plate, canned heat, or burner into their rooms.

Most students survive these youthful indiscretions; some, like Condie Cunningham, do not.

On a cold February evening in 1908, Cunningham and friends worked feverishly over a forbidden flame in their Main Hall room, trying to finish a batch of fudge. The lights-out order came and as the women hurried to extinguish the flame, Condie's nightie caught fire.

Remembering to stop, drop and roll might have saved her life, but terrified and in pain, Condie ran, making the flames worse, searing her skin. Her friends tried to help her, but the burns were too severe. Two days later, she succumbed to them.

After Condie's death, the women in the dorm noticed one of the room doors possessed an eerie likeness of her in the wood grain. In the grain, she appears to be running hard, with her hair streaming from her head.

Over the years, Main Hall residents have reported the sounds of footsteps on the run and faint cries. A few say they've caught a fleeting glimpse of a woman running across campus in a nightgown.

In Hanson Hall, a dour ghost does what it takes to keep order, even if it means giving the residents the creeps. She is never seen, but residents say they can feel her icy glare. The ghost also makes small items disappear and reappear later.

Among the other spirits, W.H. "Trummy" Trumbauer is the resident spirit of the Palmer Auditorium, and other apparitions are sometimes observed in mirrors that line the dressing room, or heard to play the organ at night. The "Lady of the Rock," can occasionally be seen near the Alpha Tau Omega house weeping over a relationship gone sour.

Arizona

University of Arizona

Some downright spooky things happen behind the stately columns at Maricopa Hall, which was completed in 1921 as a residence hall for female students. In 1992, after the hall's second major renovation, residents began noticing the fleeting image of a young woman, sometimes wearing a cloak, strolling in the basement of the hall, particularly during the quiet, early hours.

Centennial Hall, the historic performing arts center, is home to two apparently benign apparitions, although one hall worker blamed one of the ghosts for a fall in the stairwell. The first apparition bears the likeness of a male in his twenties and hangs out backstage and in the catwalks above the stage. Apparently, he's got a great sense of humor and a strange, horse-like laugh. The second apparition, a bit more evanescent than the young man, is a female with a taste for classical music.

Arkansas

Henderson State University

Originally, Henderson State was a Methodist college, and directly across the street was Ouachita Baptist University. Despite their addresses, in many ways the two schools were miles apart.

"This was a story that got started in the dorms," says Frances McLean, a 1946 Henderson State graduate. "Years and years ago, the story is that the Black Lady had been disappointed by a lover, or the usual story that you hear about these sorts of things, and she committed suicide. After that, she walks the halls of the dorm the night before the Ouachita College and Henderson State football game."

Friends of the ill-fated lovers tried to convince them their relationship was fruitless because of the doctrinal differences between their religions. The young man was a student at Ouachita; the woman was a Henderson student. The man ended the relationship, and when the woman learned he already was talking to another woman at the homecoming dance, she decided to commit suicide, although other versions of the story blame her death on melancholia – the depression that comes from a broken heart.

To this day, she hasn't recovered. Known as the Black Lady, her shadowy form walks from dorm to dorm during homecoming week looking for her lost love.

"She is a white woman dressed completely in black," McLean said.

When McLean lived in the dormitories, she said there were occasional sightings of the Black Lady. More often than not, she said, residents would hear a loud scream and one of the house parents would dash off to hear what the commotion was about.

"It was usually some woman saying 'I saw the Black Lady,'" McLean said. "No one seemed to know what caused it."

McLean said she was more scared about impersonating the Black Lady than the ghost itself. Residents were strongly discouraged from dressing up in black clothing and walking the hallways.

"Well, the powers that be said that anyone caught walking the halls or pretending to be the Black Lady would face dire consequences," McLean said. "We would be expelled or worse and you had to be very brave to attempt such a stunt. There were a couple brave people who did do that at one time or another and no one ever got caught. Something terrible was supposed to happen, so they had to be very brave to try it."

McLean said even she got involved in a plan to walk the halls as the Black Lady, but quite by accident.

"I went downstairs one day to visit a friend of mine who I had heard was going to walk the halls as the Black Lady," she said. "I was going to say 'Please, don't do it.' She was coming upstairs to see me because she had heard the same thing about me. We met on the stairs and reassured one another we had no intention of walking the halls. Years later, we had a good laugh about it."

Lyon College

A little slice of Scotland on a lush campus in Arkansas, Lyon College was founded in October 1972 as Arkansas College. The Presbyterian school's name was changed to Lyon College in February 1994.

Long before then, between 1969 and 1972, people began noticing strange things happening in the Brown Chapel and Fine Arts Building. The complex consists of the auditorium, which seats 500, a small chapel used for worship, the Bevens Music Room, and an assortment of offices, class-rooms, and practice rooms.

The auditorium became home to a bluish-green mist with a musty odor that seemed to come from a tapestry that hangs in the Bevens Music Room. The tapestry, which acquired near-legendary status, was said to have been used as a rug during the Civil War, and that a Civil War soldier actually bled to death on it. Wherever the rug traveled, its ghost was said to haunt the owner's home. When the tapestry was donated to Arkansas College, some students said they'd been able to discern bloodstains on it.

In 1985, Stan Fowler, an enterprising student in a folklore class, con-tacted the donor, Mary Barton, and cleared up some of the tapestry's his-tory. He was able to ascertain that the tale about the soldier's death on the tapestry was not true, since it was likely never used as a rug. After hanging for many years in the Barton family home in New Jersey, the tapestry was sent to Arkansas before being donated to the college.

So without the bloodstain theory, the Brown Chapel ghost's history re-mains a question mark. Students report they feel uneasy in the auditorium at times, as though they are being watched by unseen eyes. They've reported cold spots in the auditorium and chapel and say seats in the auditorium have simply fallen in front of them. Doors slam and lock by themselves in the complex, and footsteps have been heard coming from empty catwalks overhead. The prop and costume rooms seem to be inhabited by a poltergeist – or a troupe of three-year-olds – who throw items around...and vanish.

University of Central Arkansas

The ghost of Wingo Residence Hall apparently is a utility spirit – a little classic ghost, a bit of a poltergeist, and a real fan of physical comedy. Residents say the anonymous, playful spirit has been seen hovering in rooms and in the attic, opening and slamming doors, and knocking their belongings off tables and desks. She moves residents' belongings and causes window shades to open unexpectedly.

California

University of California at Berkeley

A university that laughingly refers to itself as "Berzerkley" promises to have odd and mysterious legends, and the Clark Kerr Campus of the University of California-Berkeley certainly delivers.

Let's start at the most obvious spot on campus, the Campanile. Standing 307 feet tall, it is one of Berkeley's oldest and most revered buildings. It has long withstood the school's history and stories in its eighty five years.

The tower was completed in 1917 at a cost of $144,000 and was originally named Sather Tower after its chief benefactor, Jane Sather. Sather has said one of her fondest memories involved listening to bells. Of her donation, Sather said she wanted the students at Berkeley to hear bells peal across the campus. The tower also serves as the launching pad for one of UC-Berkeley's most enduring ghost tales, concerning Pedro, a graduate student studying Sanskrit in the 1960s. When it came time for Pedro to turn in a thesis topic, he

Cal-Berkeley's Campanile is 307 feet tall and the home of Pedro, the spirit of a disgruntled graduate student. *Courtesy of the University of California-Berkeley* proposed to write not on a particular Sanskrit work, not on a particular Sanskrit sentence, but on a specific past participle and how that past participle is conjugated.

Pedro's thesis proposal was rejected and he took the news poorly. His dismay bubbled over into anger, then despair, and finally, depression. He leaped to his death from the tower and has haunted the Campanile ever since.

Students call on him for help during finals. They reason because he has carried a grudge ever since the incident, he will do anything to get back at those who shattered his dream. In 1964, a student reported being followed by a ghost as she crossed the lawn below the tower. In the late 1960s, a photographer took pictures of a phantom hand reaching out of the same grassy area.

Elsewhere on campus, room 219 of the Faculty Club has long been the center of reports of a mysterious presence. The room is known as the Tower Room because it was built as an addition to the historic Bernard Maybeck building shortly after the turn of the twentieth century.

A steep and very narrow stairway leads up to the small room with high cathedral ceilings. Dark wood paneling absorbs the afternoon sunlight as soon as it enters the room.

In one corner of the room is a queen-sized bed and chair. It was on that spot in March, 1974, when visiting professor Noriyuki Tokuda reported waking up to a man sitting on the chair looking at him.

The man disappeared and Tokuda went out to dinner with his host, Professor Chalmers Johnson and his wife. He mentioned the apparition over the meal and Johnson made sure Tokuda was moved to another room. The haunted room had been the home to Professor Henry Morse Stephens for thirty-six years. Stephens died shortly before Tokuda's visit. When Faculty Club officials described Stephens to Tokuda, he said he resembled the image that appeared in the room.

Others insist Stephens is not the ghost. They suggest that when workmen were digging the foundation for the Faculty Club in 1902, they disinterred Ohlone Indian skeletons.

But one thing is for certain.

"He's a friendly ghost," said Paul Parish, a long-time bartender at the Faculty Club. "The story has been perpetuated considerably. The story has been given legs by the *Daily Californian*, which nearly every year at Halloween runs a story about the ghost that pretty much recycles the scraps and shreds of rumors from years past so there's a kind of manufactured legend."

Parish said the building itself lends to the credence of the stories.

"The old redwood building is so creaky and ramblesome, it encourages the idea," Parish said. "And indeed things do sometimes jump off the shelves — was it a little earthquake or was it the ghost? A box of espresso cups just fell off a shelf in the closet last week, and I thought about the ghost. There was no explaining it aside from a tremor in the building, but it is a very flexible building and if they move the furniture in the banquet room upstairs, it sounds like elephants stomping around."

California State University Long Beach

Students and campus employees say the university's occasionally foggy student union is operated by unseen hands.

Those hands open and close doors within the center at night when the exterior doors are locked and no one is inside. Those unseen hands press the buttons on the elevator, taking riders to floors they never intended to visit. No one's reported an apparition and no unexplained noises have been heard, but the strange fog that pops up occasionally and the goofy elevators and doors are spooky enough to make some folks wonder.

California State University Stanislaus

When the Stockton Developmental Center was closed in 1996, the state moved quickly to transform the center grounds to a satellite campus for Cal State Stanislaus.

The complex was originally developed as a state hospital for the mentally ill and was later used as a center for training the developmentally disabled. The first building on the site was completed in 1853, but of the fifty six buildings on the 102-acre site at the time of the center's closure, all were built between 1870 and 1979. The site was reopened as the university's Stockton Center in 1997, and already has a resident ghost, albeit left over from the center's days as a mental hospital.

Among the first buildings to be pressed into service for the Stockton Center was the Acacia Court – formerly lodging, workshops, and classrooms for the residents, and before that, the patients. Legend has it that some of the attendants and nurses lived in apartments on the building's third floor and one of the nurses who lived there became overwhelmed by the despair and hopelessness of the mentally ill during those dark times.

When she could bear it no longer, she hung herself. She appears in the third-floor windows every once and again and in the meantime, walks the halls, checking on her patients.

The building's quick transition also meant many of the architectural vestiges were left as they were, which tends to give a few students the creeps. The basement morgue has been sealed, but the small windows and other reminders still exist. And just to keep the atmosphere, the hall doorways occasionally slam on breezeless days.

University of LaVerne

A pair of deaths – one a tragic accident, the other a suicide – help explain the strange happenings at Founders Hall. People working alone say they hear doors slamming and the sound of someone running in the building. Those noises, plus various others, are attributed to a despondent audio-visual director who committed suicide there in 1978, and also to Professor Gladdys Muir, who died after tumbling down the stairs in 1967.

San Diego State University

Zura Hall is the university's oldest residence hall and the scene of a grisly 1974 rape and murder. But while the victim was a female (and her attacker was apprehended and convicted of the crime), the apparitions most often seen in the hall are males. On some of the hall's floors, the disembodied voice of a man has beckoned residents. One bathroom rings with the sound of pinging, as if an unseen hand were dropping a hard, bouncy object on the floors. The hazy figure of a slightly built man has also been reported silently stalking the hallways and lounges.

University of California at Santa Cruz

Sarah Cowell, the youngest daughter of the influential limestone broker, land and cattle baron, and recluse Henry Cowell, perished in 1903 in an accident on the family's ranch. Sarah was killed and a servant was injured when the horse got spooked and threw them from their buggy. Henry Cowell had told his daughter not to take the buggy out, but she disobeyed his order. Brokenhearted, Henry Cowell died later that year. Sarah's sisters Isabella and Helen refused to ever return to the ranch property again, but Sarah apparently does. The Cowell ranch became the site for the University of California at Santa Cruz, and Sarah's ghost occasionally makes an appearance.

Colorado

Metropolitan State College at Denver
University of Colorado at Denver
Community College of Denver

It should seem only fair that the Sigi's Cabaret, in the Tivoli Student Union, which serves students from a trio of colleges, should be haunted by a trio of ghosts. The troika includes the specters of an American Indian and pioneers from the nineteenth and early twentieth centuries.

The three are not very active as ghosts go, but who has time to haunt when you've got a place like the Tivoli to stay in? Built in a converted brewery, it functions as a combination student union, shopping mall, and entertainment complex.

The Rocky Mountain Brewery first occupied the land, starting in 1859, and provided huge amounts of a cold, golden beverage for the hard-working men who dug and panned for gold in the fields. Business went flat in the latter part of the twentieth century and the brewery was closed in 1969. In 1973, the deserted building was resurrected due to its listing on the National Register for Historic Places, which prevented demolition of the brewery. After moving through a succession of owners, students of the three colleges, which comprise the Auraria Higher Education Center, voted to transform the historic old brewery into the student union and retail emporium. The complex began construction in 1992 and the refurbished complex opened in 1994.

The haunting threesome has made their presence known in small ways. Staff from a restaurant that set its tables up at night for the next day's guests sometimes returned to find the tables in disarray, but each time, building security detected no activity and there was no evidence of anyone entering the building.

The trio of specters are not the only ones haunting the building. In the Multicultural Lounge, a well-dressed but forlorn little girl has been observed by many. Each time someone attempts to approach her, she simply vanishes.

Connecticut

Yale University

The Newberry Memorial Organ in Yale University's Woolsey Hall, designed by the famed architects John Carriere and Thomas Hastings. *Courtesy of Yale University*

How could the university that is home to the Order of Skull and Bones, the super-secret society for the offspring of the power elite, not be riddled with ghosts?

Truth is, Yale ghost stories are few, but the Gothic secret societies that flourish there provide a wealth of stories that are ghostly, ghastly, and mysterious. Because they are secret and little information leaks out, the rumors are probably more titillating than the truth, but we'll never know.

The oldest of the societies is Skull and Bones, which counts among its numbers George H.W. Bush (Class of '48) and George W. Bush (Class of '68). There are several other secret societies such Berzilius, Skull and Keys, Book and Snake, and Wolf's Head, but none has cachet to match Skull and Bones. The more prominent of the organizations meet in windowless buildings on campus or nearby called tombs. Their initiation rituals are reported to utilize human bones and are said to include requiring initiates to lie naked in coffins.

Skull and Bones, for example, traces its roots back to 1832. It taps fifteen members a year, never more, never less. The midnight ritual involves a somber, silent procession to the rooms of the selected individuals. The leader carries a human skull and bone and quietly says to each person chosen: "Skull and Bones, do you accept?"

These societies, with their secret rituals, arcane traditions, and ancient lore bring initiates into an incubator that prepares them for their roles in the bedrock of business, the arts, government, and the upper crust of society.

For the rest of us, Yale has a supply of ghost stories, too.

Woolsey Hall was designed by an influential New York architectural firm headed by John Carriere and Thomas Hastings. The 1901 hall was part of a grandiose three-building complex commemorating the university's bicentennial. The crowning glory of the hall was the Newberry Memorial Organ, which the university's Institute for Sacred Music boasts is "one of the most famous romantic organs in the world."

Harry B. Jepson, the university's organist, solicited the Newberry family's assistance in refurbishing the organ and received their support for renovations in 1916 and 1926. The 1926 alterations did not go well. The two firms working on the organ did not work well together and tensions ebbed throughout. Jepson was forced into retirement in 1940 and died, embittered, in 1952. Frank Bozyan, a successor to Jepson, reluctantly retired in the seventies. Within six months, he was dead. Both men had learned that the stewardship of a great instrument such as the organ requires the same devotion one has for a child or a family. When separated from the organ, both men felt alone. Jepson, who lived near the hall, never set foot in the building after he was forced into retirement.

Some say Jepson's spirit watches out over Woolsey Hall and others have claimed to hear music flowing spontaneously from the famed organ. Visitors say they feel as though their moves are being scrutinized and find themselves looking behind them just to be sure they aren't being followed. Jepson, like many others before him, learned that secrecy rules at Yale.

Delaware

University of Delaware

The call rang out as he sat on the hard wooden bench, trying to absorb the day's lessons. As soon as he heard the words, he knew he had to go.

It was 1777. The United States was in its infancy and it was a time for brave men to step forward to defend the young nation and the ideals for which it stood.

A combined force of 16,000 soldiers had come ashore at the Elk River in Cecil County, Maryland. Twelve thousand of the intruders were British, the rest Hessian mercenaries.

As soon as he could slip away, he left his school – the Rev. Dr. Francis Alison's Academy of New Ark – on Main Street in Newark.

The academy for boys had opened in 1743 in Alison's home and eventually moved into the three-story brick building.

"Now a part of the University of Delaware and called the Academy Building, the tower or cupola is believed to be haunted," says Ed Okonowicz, a writer for the University of Delaware and also a popular and prolific writer of ghost stories and regional history. Okonowicz owns Myst and Lace Publishers and leads many ghost walks and cemetery tours throughout the Delmarva area.

"As the local legend goes," Okonowicz says, "a young student of the academy responded to the call for volunteers by leaving school and joining an American unit that was camping at nearby Iron Hill, a small elevated site that is nowadays adjacent to Interstate 95."

The hill was being used as a reconnaissance outpost to keep tabs on the British troops and the Hessians.

"When the father of the young lad found out about his son's decision, the parent went to Iron Hill and grabbed the boy by the ear, pulling him away from the campfire and leading him back to his studies at the New Ark Academy," Okonowicz said.

The indignity and embarrassment the young man suffered had been crushing. He felt he could show his face to no one, so "on the night of his return to school, the student climbed the ladder leading to the wooden watch tower and hung himself," Okonowicz said.

His body was found the next morning, yet his ghost remains there, more than 225 years later. The young man's father's wish was that the boy would remain in school, and he has…seemingly forever.

District of Columbia

Georgetown University

The university that was the site of William Peter Blatty's 1971 thriller *The Exorcist* is a quart low when it comes to hauntings.

Blatty, a former Georgetown student, used his memories of the university, particularly a flight of outdoor stairs from Prospect Street to M Street, for his book. They're known today as "The Exorcist Stairs." Blatty took details from a Maryland exorcism he'd read about as a basis for the story, and added his own embellishments, such as changing the victim from a male to a female, and setting the events in Georgetown. The book sold more than thirteen million copies. The 1973 film earned Blatty an Oscar for Best Screenplay.

The most often told ghost story on campus is that of haunted Healy Hall.

At the junction of O and 37th Streets, Healy Hall is the building people encounter when they enter through the university's main gates. It's a breathtaking building, designed by the firm of Smithmeyer and Peltz, who also designed the Library of Congress. The building was completed in 1875 and dedicated to honor Patrick Healy, the university president from 1873 to 1882. Healy held the distinction of being the first black man to become president of an American university.

In 1971, Healy Hall was entered into the National Register of Historic Places.

The clock tower that rises from the middle of the building is visible from nearly everywhere on campus, and has proved alluring to daredevils. Stealing the hands of the clock used to be considered the ultimate Georgetown athletic conquest.

The clock tower is now sealed off to students, but legend persists that the ghost of a Jesuit who slipped and fell to his death while setting the clock's hands near the start of the twentieth century stays within. Believers insist that, should any foolhardy students manage to run the gauntlet of locks and barred doors, the spirit who paces the top of the tower will watch over them.

Gallaudet University

Gallaudet is the only liberal arts university in the world established to meet the needs of deaf and hearing-impaired students. It is especially ironic, then, that what gave up the ghost of Gallaudet was the rattling sound of the second-floor shutters at the Edward Miner Gallaudet Residence. The Gallaudet Residence, official home of the university president, looks as though it came right off the set of a horror flick. Picture it: twenty rooms, Victorian Gothic. It is a National Historic Trust building, and a profoundly eerie one at that. The home was built in 1869 and named to honor the university's founding president.

When the rattling began, campus police were dispatched twice that night, and both times they came away empty-handed but perplexed. People in the house have said they sense a presence, and some individuals with normal hearing have noted the sounds of footsteps and doors opening and closing.

Florida

Brevard Community College

Joe the Ghost watches over the historic Cocoa Village Playhouse on the Florida Space Coast

The Historic Cocoa Village Playhouse is a rare gem on the high-tech Space Coast and Joe the Ghost makes sure it stays that way.

First known as the Aladdin Theatre, the Italian Renaissance-style building had been constructed in 1924. In the 1940s, it was converted to a filmhouse called the State Theatre. In 1984, BCC acquired the building (and Joe) from the city and restored the building as part of the Brevard Cultural Alliance Theaters. Another theater in the alliance, the Henegar Center for the Arts, also is haunted. The resident apparition there is named Jonathan.

In 1989, the 500-seat Historic Cocoa Village Playhouse began offering a variety of performances and events featuring a mix of community performers and professionals. The theater was added to the National Register for Historic Places in 1991.

"Joe was an electrical worker in the theater while it was a movie house back in the 1940s," said Jeff Lowe, a former employee.

Lowe first encountered Joe as he and his colleagues took a moment's rest after the completion of a show.

"I was leaning against the stage looking up at the balcony and the others were sitting in seats facing the stage," he said. "I noticed that there was a man in the balcony standing in the back row. Being new to the playhouse then, I did not give it much thought.

"Moments later, the director said we all needed to go home and get some sleep, and as we headed out, I mentioned that I thought someone else was still in the theater. I was assured that we were the only ones there and was then rushed out of the door so the alarm could be set for the night."

Lowe didn't think much about the incident for a few days.

"I heard one of the kids in the show say something about Joe the ghost," he said. "At that time, I got a very strange feeling on the back of my neck like static electricity.

"Wanting to know more, I went to the sound man, who had been working at the Cocoa Village Playhouse for several years and described to him exactly what I had seen and asked if he knew anything about the ghost. He laughed a little and told me to follow him up to the balcony.

"Repeating back to me what I had told him about the figure walking across the back row of the balcony and directly through the door to the booth area, he pointed out that behind the back row and the door was a four-foot-high wall separating the two. In the dark, I could not see the wall, but there was no doubt that whomever or whatever I saw that night had passed through it effortlessly. I thought I was going to faint.

"I am not a firm believer in ghosts," Lowe says. "But I know I saw something that night I will never be able to explain."

Broward Community College

Omar makes his home at Broward Community College's Fine Arts Theatre, the smaller of two performing arts venues at the college's A. Hugh Adams Central Campus

An unassertive ghost named Omar occasionally pops up to tease drama students and technical crew members working on productions at the A. Hugh Adams Central Campus Fine Arts Theatre. He's not known to join the audience but he's been reported darting about backstage occasionally, leaving cold spots behind and making staff members and students aware – and wary – of his presence.

Flagler College

The Flagler College main entrance on King Street. This photo was shot from the front door of city hall, across King Street.

Exterior view of Flagler College's Great Rotunda, where Henry Flagler's body lay in state before his funeral

Railroad magnate Henry Morrison Flagler's entrepreneurial spirit helped transform Florida from a swampy wonderland to a progressive state, and his ghost and those of his second and third wives are reputed to appear at Flagler College and at Whitehall, the Flagler family home in Palm Beach.

Flagler first came to St. Augustine for the comfort and health benefits for his ill wife, Mary Harkness. She was accompanied by a full-time caregiver named Ida Alice Shourds. After Mary's death, Flagler married Shourds, but learned quickly enough that while his first wife's problems had been physical, his second wife's maladies were mental. Before long, Ida Alice required commitment to an asylum and remained there the remainder of her life. During Ida Alice's commitment, Flagler met Mary Lily Kenan, who was vacationing at the first of the hotels Flagler built in St. Augustine, the Ponce de Leon. Mary Lily was a lovely, poised young woman from a prominent, influential North Carolina family.

The attraction was mutual, but Flagler had a problem. Divorce was not permitted in Florida at the time, so he had his cronies in the state legislature pull a few strings for him. They created a bill that permitted persons to divorce if their spouses were incurably mentally ill. The "Flagler Divorce Law," as it became known, opened the door to his marriage to Mary Lily in 1901. At the time of the marriage, Mary Lily was thirty-four, Flagler was seventy-one.

Flagler moved on to build a grand resort in Palm Beach for the fabulously wealthy, and Mary Lily, whose social graces were more polished than his, proved to be an excellent wife and an asset to his business.

Flagler suffered a fall on the grand staircase at Whitehall, his Palm Beach home. Already in declining health at the time, his health deteriorated quickly. He moved into a bungalow alongside the beach and in 1913, at age eighty-three, he died.

He originally was to have been buried in West Palm Beach's Woodlawn Cemetery, a pineapple field he converted to a graveyard, but in 1911, the city of West Palm Beach tried to annex Palm Beach and Flagler, angered at the gesture, canceled his plans.

After his death, his family followed his amended plan and transported his remains back to St. Augustine for funeral and internment. His body was placed in the rotunda of the Ponce de Leon and mourners began somberly gathering for the procession to the Memorial Presbyterian Church, which is located on the block behind the Ponce de Leon. As the somber group assembled in silence, all the doors of the rotunda suddenly slammed shut. An electrified buzz filled the room, followed by a few moments' confusion, but attendants quickly restored order and decorum and the funeral procession began.

Later that day, a janitor mopping the rotunda noticed that one of the many tiles that make up the floor bore a distinct resemblance to Flagler. He had mopped the floor many times and had never noticed the tile.

Flagler is interred with his first wife Mary, a daughter, and a granddaughter. Mary Lily, his third wife, remarried and died under questionable circumstances; many people suggested foul play. She is buried at Oaklawn Cemetery in Wilmington, North Carolina. Her ghost and Flagler's are said to reside at Whitehall.

For years, students have said Flagler's and Ida's benign ghosts wander Ponce de Leon Hall.

Flagler College was created as a liberal arts college for women in 1968. Before long, it became coed and enjoys an excellent reputation for its educational programs. The college emphatically denies it is inhabited by ghosts and especially attempts to debunk the oft-published tale that the top floor of Ponce de Leon Hall is locked because it was where Flagler's mistress committed suicide. There was no mistress nor any suicide there.

"The fourth floor is off limits only because the center of the floor is unstable," says Laurin Bosse, the college's director of public information.

Stable parts of the floor house furniture from the old hotel, which members of the college's Students in Free Enterprise organization hope to replicate and offer for sale.

The college does plan to stabilize and use the fourth floor in the future, but has a few other rehabilitation projects on the docket first.

Florida Atlantic University

A beautiful, modern campus just a few miles from Boca Raton beach, Florida Atlantic University might look like Suntan U. Established in 1964, FAU has proven itself as an outstanding, progressive university in a world-class setting. Though the campus is sun-swept and modern, it's a university with more history than it may be apparent on the surface. During World War II, the land on which the university was built was one of several air training bases in South Florida. Some of the old runways still are visible

With its modern lines, pastel paint, and tropical landscaping, Florida Atlantic University's University Theatre doesn't seem to have haunted potential.

and a few of the old war-era buildings are scattered on the outskirts of the college.

On its eastern side is the Dorothy Schmidt Performing Arts Center, home of the University Theatre, formerly known as the Esther B. Griswold Theatre, built in 1966. Deep in the dark recesses of the theater, in the area where hydraulic equipment has been installed to raise and lower the stage, people who have been alone there at night say they feel they are not really alone at all.

When they're working at night, they say they can distinctly hear distant voices in the building and doors closing in the theater above. Still, when they go to check, they find the doors all in their proper positions, the building locked and empty.

"They say the presence is distinctly female, very benign and they've been aware of it for more than ten years," said one staff member. "They said they get the feeling that it's her habitat."

Florida State University

Cawthon Hall is one of several residence halls at Florida State University bordering Landis Green at the center of the campus.

The Chi Omega sorority house on Jefferson Street, where Ted Bundy paid his fateful visit in January 1978.

Set in beautiful rolling hills and liberally dotted with oak and pecan trees on its campus, Florida State University almost seems more a part of Georgia than Florida, but the Sunshine State's capital city and its major university are home to plenty of haunts.

Gilchrist Hall is where the spirit of a homesick young music major is said to live. On particularly still nights, when the weather is crisp and the sky is inky and dotted with stars, one can occasionally hear the soft strains of flute music coming from the area where the halls of the T-shaped building meet.

Walking from Gilchrist Hall along the side of Landis Green toward the Robert Manning Strozier Library, one encounters Cawthon Hall, another residence reputed to have a ghostly past. Cawthon is the site of what is probably the university's longest-running ghost tale: the story of a coed who was struck by lightning while she sunbathed at "tar beach" on the roof. Like many ghost legends, it doesn't let truth get in the way of a good story. *FSView* and the *Florida Flambeau* checked out the legend and found that the hall's construction was completed after the event was to have occurred. A bolt of lightning did strike the hall's roof in 1958, however, but a student sunbathing there was not injured.

That's not to say Cawthon Hall isn't home to unexplained phenomena. Students leave their dorms tidy and with the lights out and return to find the lights on and the rooms mussed up. Other say channels on their TV set change by themselves.

The most compelling tale students have reported is sighting a hazy, floating female figure clad in green who they have named "Tissie". Some believe Tissie is the hall's namesake, Sarah Landrum Cawthon, former dean of Florida State College for Women. The dorm was completed March 15, 1948, the sixth anniversary of Cawthon's death.

On Jefferson Street, several hundred feet from the edge of Landis Green, shaded under live oak and pecan trees, and just down the street from The Sweet Shop, is the Chi Omega house. There, late on January 14th or early the 15th, 1978, Ted Bundy carried out a grisly rampage that left two students dead and two more severely beaten. Bundy, who was living in a rooming house on College Avenue a few blocks away, slipped into the sorority house and attacked four of the residents. Two women – roommates Lisa Levy and Margaret Bowman – died from their injuries. One the way back to his apartment he attacked yet another woman, who fortunately survived her injuries.

There have never been any ghost sightings at the Chi-O house, but residents say that at times they feel a peculiar presence there.

Bundy was executed in Florida's gas chamber in Starke on January 24, 1989, but not for the Chi Omega killings, of which he also had been convicted. The death warrant carried out was for the murder of Kimberly Leach, a twelve year old from Lake City.

Nova Southeastern University

The modern Leo Goodwin Sr. residence hall is across the street from BCC's Fine Arts Theatre. Perhaps the dorm is Omar's home.

There are no tall columns at Leo Goodwin Sr. Hall, no droopy Spanish moss, no cemetery nearby. The modern, pastel-colored 296-student residence hall was opened during the 1992-93 school year, but already has acquired its own ghost.

"One of my sorority sisters was a residence assistant and she told me Goodwin was haunted," says Dania Rivero, Class of '94.

The dorm was named to honor a major benefactor of the college, and isn't the kind of dwelling normally associated with ghost tales.

"When they were getting ready for the fall term one year, my friend was setting up the beds, the tables and chairs and putting everything in order for the students to arrive," Rivero said. "When she was doing her final check, she found a couple of the rooms rearranged — and no one else, other than the RAs, had access to them."

The ghost apparently likes some of the finer things in life.

"My friend said she was getting complaints from a student who thought her roommate was stealing from her because the expensive perfume her mom bought her was getting lower and lower in the bottle and at times she'd smell the perfume in the room," Rivero said. "Once, in the middle of the night she was awakened and saw a shadowy figure at her bedside. She thought the ghost was putting on her perfume. She said she hid under the covers and didn't look out until morning."

Ringling School of Art and Design

For years, they've called her Mary Ringling, though Ringling was most certainly not her last name. She was attractive but years of prostitution gave her features a hard edge. She lived and practiced the oldest profession in relative anonymity in an apartment building a few blocks off U.S. 41, better known as Tamiami Trail, which runs through Sarasota.

Sarasota was an intriguing place to be in the 1920s. A few miles north on 41, circus magnate John Ringling had begun wintering in the area in 1909. In 1925, he and his wife Mable began work on Ca d'Zan, their Venetian Gothic mansion. In 1927, he brought his circus to winter at Sarasota and began work on a museum to house his substantial art collection. He also invested heavily in home construction in the area.

The Ringlings were at first snubbed by the wealthy northerners who wintered there, but were eventually accepted into local society. There was no room in society for Mary, who felt as though she were invisible. She knew she would never attend their fancy parties, premieres, and regattas. Although she might come in contact with some of the men who attended those events, she knew she would never go to them on their arms. As Sarasota grew more prominent and prosperous, her depression grew deeper.

Finally, she felt she had endured enough. Legend has it she shot herself on the stairwell between the second and third floors. Few knew about the incident and even fewer cared.

In 1931, the Ringling School of Art and Design opened to its first class of seventy-five students. As the school grew, it acquired buildings throughout the neighborhood along the Tamiami Trail and restored them. One of those buildings was the apartment house where Mary had lived and worked. It was converted to a women's dormitory now known as the Keating Complex.

Not long after students began settling in, they began hearing noises, particularly in the stairwell. Sometimes they'd catch a glimpse of a woman in the dorm window or on the stairs, and hear the gentle swish of her long dress as she hurried off. After they'd learned the history of the building and its ill-fated resident, they understood what was happening. They've never been particularly scared by her.

"It's just Mary," they'd laugh and say. "Just Mary."

In the spirit world, as it had been in her lifetime, Mary remains nearly invisible.

University of Florida

Students say a depressed young woman who leaped to her death from one of the Beaty Towers, part of the Towers/Jennings Area at the Gainesville university, is back among them again.

Beaty Towers was designed by architect Forrest Kelly and was dedicated in June 1971. It was named to honor Robert Calder Beaty, who served as a dean and in other roles in his thirty-six years there.

The woman who haunts the twin high-rise dorms seems peaceful and is usually quiet as she strolls the hallways there, but if she slips into a room, she's sure to rearrange things.

University of Tampa

Compared to the grand, spacious performing arts complexes many colleges and universities operate, the David Falk Theatre of the University of Tampa is a bit more modest, but still a special place.

The theater is an 835-seat drama boutique and has two things that make it unique. The first is a magnificent history. The second is the gentle ghost of Bessie Snavely.

The theater is across Kennedy Boulevard from the Plant Hall, the university's signature building with its beautiful silver minarets. Plant Hall was built by Henry B. Plant between 1888 and 1891 as the five-story, 511-room Tampa Bay Hotel, the finest example of Moorish architecture in the United States. Located in the heart of Tampa's downtown, it was the showplace hotel for the city and held onto that role until 1933, when the hotel was transformed into the University of Tampa.

Early in the 1930s, what is now the Falk Theatre was called the Park Theatre. It had opened as a vaudeville theater and later became a road house – a theater that plays host to touring companies. Actress Bessie Snavely and her husband worked there, but his flirtatious nature had caused Bessie to fall into a funk. That funk deepened when he left her for another member of the company.

Theater companies are like large, extended families, and in hers, Bessie could see everyone looking at her, pointing. Some laughed, some sympathized, but they looked at her differently. Finally she could no longer face her cheeks burning from humiliation or stand the shame. She hung herself in her dressing room, a room that now often seems far colder than the rest of the building.

Bessie apparently was a kind and thoughtful woman. Spared the indignity of her husband's unfaithfulness, Bessie now roams Falk Theatre tidying things up, closing doors and keeping the crew members from harm. Occasionally a crew member or actor catches a glimpse of her peering from the lighting booth or elsewhere in the theater, watching a rehearsal or performance. The show must go on and Bessie Snavely helps keep the wheels of efficiency greased.

Georgia

Berry College

Martha Berry was an educational visionary who opened a school for rural boys in 1902, and added one for girls in 1909. As the students grew older and the school's reputation spread, it took on the challenge of post-secondary education with a junior college in 1926, a four-year college in 1930, and a graduate school 1972.

The school is a Ponderosa-sized layout, with two campuses (Main and Mountain) spread over 28,000 acres. A lot can happen at a place that large, and Chris Duke took notice.

"I became interested in Berry's ghost history after hearing many, many first-hand stories from other people," said Duke, a member of the Class of 2005 and a staff writer for *The Campus Carrier*, Berry's student newspaper. "These were not just reports from the occasional student, but these were also from respected professors and alumni, including some people I had known long before I went to Berry College. I do not claim ghosts exist or do not exist, but something has to be going on if this many people – and trustworthy people at that – are seeing things. I'm just trying to figure out what that something is."

One of Berry's most often-repeated tales occurs not in a classroom, theatre or dorm, but along a stretch of roadway.

"There are many stories about the Green Lady, but most of these are corrupted and unreliable," Duke says. "Many students have seen a green mist on Stretch Road, which is the only road connecting the Mountain Campus to the Main Campus. Some students have seen a small female appear out of the mist. She is slightly green like the mist and is reported to be wearing period dress from 1900 to 1920 or so. Some reports say she has no eyes and other reports say she beckons to any witnesses."

Another special spot on campus is the House o' Dreams, a stone cottage atop Lavendar Mountain that was given to Martha Berry in 1926 to commemorate the twenty-fifth anniversary of her schools. The cottage, with a commanding view over the campus, was lovingly created. Faculty, staff and students provided the labor. Using materials from Lavendar Mountain, the students constructed the furniture and wove fabrics used in the interior décor. The landscaping, complete with fruit trees and berry patches, added the finishing touch.

"Students and workers have seen many lights and the apparition of a woman, although this does not appear to be Martha Berry," Duke said. "She seems to be the spirit of a woman who died in a plane crash."

Those who have seen the apparition describe her as toothless. A caretaker and an interested student once dug through the rubble of the plane crash after the authorities finished their search. Among their discoveries was a piece of dental work.

Oak Hill, Martha Berry's mansion, is reported to have windows that open and close themselves, and alarm systems that turn on without apparent reason.

Ford Hall, used for musical events, drama productions, and campus events, along with Morton-Lemley Hall dorm also have been the locales of sightings.

LaGrange College

The ghost of a Confederate officer in full dress uniform has been reported pacing the halls of the second floor of Smith Hall.

University of Georgia

How 'bout them ghosts?

Few college football programs have the tradition or the devotion the Bulldogs enjoy. The university's ghostly legacy might be influenced by the presence of the Old Athens Cemetery, between Baldwin Hall and the University of Georgia Art School on Jackson Street, where cold spots have been reported over the years.

The most persistent tale is of Lustrat House, but there are others.

Lustrat House, built in 1847, was one of several faculty homes constructed on the campus. Its was named for Joseph Lustrat, a native of Paris who was educated at The Sorbonne and served many years as the head of the university's Department of Romance Languages. He lived in the home with his wife and three daughters from 1904 until his death in 1927.

Before Lustrat, the two-story, eight-room brick building was home to Professor Charles Morris, who was angered when the home was moved from its original location at the site of the Georgia Museum of Art in 1903. Morris was angered by the decision to move the home and left, but is said to have returned to the building after his mortal years and has been reported sitting at his desk and next to the fireplace, attired in a CSA uniform, working on paperwork.

Lustrat House served as the president's office through mid 2000 and now is home to the university's Department of Legal Affairs.

Other haunted activity on campus is said to include:

• Joseph E. Brown Hall, named for the former four-time governor and U.S. Senator, where the apparition of a young man has been reported looking in…and looking out. Now the home for the university's Department of Germanic and Slavic Languages, the building once served as a dormitory and a student committed suicide there.

• Alpha Gamma Delta sorority house, which ironically looks like a three-layer wedding cake. It was constructed in 1896 and was to have been the site of a Southern belle's finest moment, but instead was the site of her death when she committed suicide after her fiancee failed to turn up for their wedding. Alpha Gamma Delta's chapter opened in 1924 on campus.

Hawai'i

University of Hawai'i at Manoa

Neither gods nor spirits – not even vengeful ones – frighten Hawaiians. The Hawaiian islands are loaded with them, from the eerie Night Marchers, who strike you dead if you step in their way, to the playful but industrious menehunes, the tempestuous volcano goddess Pele, and many more.

The women who live at Frear Hall say that on calm, balmy nights, the sweet fragrance of old-fashioned perfume wafts down the hallways of their dorm.

A resident once reported that late one Saturday night as she headed up to her room, she passed an elderly woman on the stairway. She noticed little about the woman except her age, that she was dressed in white, and that she carried a ring of keys. Several weeks later, the staff hung a portrait of Mary Dillingham Frear, an early member of the Board of Regents, in a common room of the dorm. When the young resident took a look, she felt her stomach fall and the blood drain from her face. The woman with the keys who had passed her on the stairway was the same woman.

"I have not had first-hand experience with Ms. Frear," says Ku'ulei Pau, residential life coordinator for Student Housing Services. "But [I] have heard many stories about her being seen, her perfume being smelled throughout the building, as well as the sound of her walking throughout the building."

When Pau lived in Hale Kahawai, a dorm that accommodates 156 women in double rooms with floors accessible only by stairs, she had a ghostly experience.

"The women during my time of residing there nicknamed him Herman," she said. "He resided on the second floor of the all-woman hall. The story I got on this ghost is that he lived at Hale Kahawai during a summer session and fell in love with a local haole (non-Hawaiian) girl. They dated during the summer, and when he returned to his mainland home, he was involved in a tragic accident and his ghost returned to Hale Kahawai."

Herman always was the perfect gentleman, she said.

"The women never expressed fear of Herman, I guess, because he was a friendly ghost," she said. "He played games with the women by moving items in the room while they were studying and removing accessories from their hair."

If Herman ever craved a little male company, there was always George, the other ghost in the four-story dorm.

"George was the other ghost we had at HK," Pau said. "He resides on the fourth floor. He would move items around on the floor and turn room lights on and off in rooms that were unoccupied."

Windward Community College

Bob is a benign and occasionally playful spirit who lives in the Iolani Building, an arts and science building at the Kaneohe college, which was a state hospital before it became part of the University of Hawai'i's community college system in 1972.

Probably a patient during his mortal years, Bob likes order and is known to tidy up and put away items left out by others.

Idaho

Boise State University

What now serves as the university's Communication Building formerly was the Student Union and home to the Subal Theatre, where a crestfallen student named Dina ran after being stood up on a date. It's there, too, where she took her life.

Since Dina's demise, things haven't been the same there.

Kathleen Craven, the university's public relations officer, said she's heard many of the stories about Dina and has concluded "even skeptics have had experiences that couldn't be explained."

Dina's playful antics have included leaving footprints on freshly painted scenery, loud footsteps, and knocks on doors late at night.

In one case, two student thespians working in the theater late at night heard footsteps at the top of the stairs, heading to the costume shop. Knowing they were the only people in the theater, they followed the sound of the steps up the steep stairway to the shop's only entry. The footsteps stopped abruptly as they heard the door open. Then, they heard only silence. They searched the costume shop thoroughly and found nothing.

Since the building's transformation into the Communication Building, Dina's pranks have involved more run-of-the-mill antics, including fiddling with the light switches and making those loud, telltale footsteps.

Illinois

Eastern Illinois University

A ghost named Mary haunts Pemberton Hall, a residence for women. According to the legend, Mary is the spirit of a counselor bludgeoned to death by a crazed custodian in the 1920s.

The murder took place on the dorm's third floor. Despite the frenzied incident that caused her death, Mary is not a menacing poltergeist. Rather, she appears to be a motherly spirit who looks after the young women in her former residence hall.

Her spirit glides silently from room to room, making sure doors are locked, televisions and stereos are off. She generally acts like a house-mother from beyond.

"I don't know if you'd call her friendly," said Vicki Woodard, a university spokesperson.

EIU students have a strong knowledge of Mary. She had been practicing the piano late at night in Pemberton's fourth-floor music room. Mary was one of several students who remained at the old dorm during spring break in the early twenties. The maid's quarters on the fourth floor had been opened early that night to facilitate the janitor's cleaning, and explaining his access to the floor. The janitor lugged an ax onto the floor with him and spotted Mary. He attacked her viciously and chased her as she lurched, injured through the halls, attempting to flee. She clawed at the door to her room, desperately seeking help from her roommate, who was too terrified to render assistance. Mary collapsed in a pool of blood in the hallway outside her door. Her lifeless body was discovered the next morning by her roommate. The ax-wielding janitor was never apprehended.

Mary's spirit has never left "Pem" Hall. She still keeps up her nightly rounds, checking windows, turning off lights, and keeping things tidy.

Bradley University

The Hartmann Center for the Performing Arts is home to a ghostly cast of characters who lurk behind its dark windows, ready to terrorize the unwary. The first is believed to be the ghost of a former coach who killed himself when the building served as a gymnasium. He appears as a cloudy image outlining a male figure and is often accompanied by the scent of cigar smoke.

The second is the ghost of a woman who roams through the center's gallery and sometimes blows the lights out there.

The Harper/Wyckoff residence hall is home to a playful spirit who fiddles with the buttons of the hall elevator and makes noises throughout the building.

University of Illinois

Over the years, the university's English Building has been the focal point of a variety of ghostly tales, particularly from the days when it served as a self-contained women's dorm, equipped with living quarters, classrooms, offices, kitchens, and more.

However, an excursion through college records shows the tales of suicidal students and other campus violence are without merit. It also is ground zero for at least one contemporary urban legend. In it, a student returns to her room at night to pick up an item, and leaves again. To keep from waking her sleeping roommate, she tiptoes into the room in the dark, takes the items, and slips out silently. The next morning when she returns, she opens the door to find the roommate brutally murdered, and on the mirror, written in the roommate's own lipstick, these words: "Aren't you glad you didn't turn on the light?"

The building was designed in the New Colonial style by New York City-based architects Charles Follen McKim, William Rutherford Mead and Stanford White in 1905. The firm of McKim, Mead and White was responsible for many of the era's major buildings, including the Boston Public Library, Newport Casino and Pennsylvania Station in New York.

The English Building has undergone several renovations over the years and now as a classroom and office building it is bright, spacious, airy, and thoroughly modern inside. Still, even if the tales of ghosts and horror are untrue, inquiring minds want to know what's the source of those noises on the third floor? The sounds include doors slamming, footsteps, and lights, computers, and other appliances that turn themselves on and off.

Indiana

University of Notre Dame

The University of Notre Dame is one of America's legendary football colleges and one of its golden gridiron greats, George Gipp, still haunts his old room in Washington Hall. The building now serves as the home theatre for the university's drama club. Gipp's visits now are to the stage and the green room backstage.

"I have collected about twenty-five to thirty ghost stories over the past few years and several of them center on Washington Hall," says Rev. Robert A. Austgen, retired chaplain for the Notre Dame health services. "Not only the Gipp (story), but many others, too."

The legend of Gipp – better known as The Gipper – is perhaps the most popular. Never one to follow the rules, especially those having to do with curfew, Gipp devoted his energies to breaking the rules and evading those whose job it was to enforce them.

One evening too many, he stayed out past curfew.

"It was a cold night in early December and refusing to incur the wrath, Gipp slept outside on the steps of Washington Hall," Austgen said. "On December 14th, 1920, Gipp died of pneumonia. Knute Rockne brought him back with his famous 'win one for The Gipper' speech. Our housekeepers on their way back to their 4 a.m. check-in swear that they still encounter Gipp on the steps.

"Of course we at Notre Dame all hope that The Gipper might be back for a snap or two," Austgen said.

Some ghostly legends predate Gipp's legendary all-America 1920 season, but he still gets credit for the legend of the waving tombstones. Two students were returning to campus from South Bend in the wee hours. It was so late, Austgen said, the trolleys had stopped running and the two young men were forced to walk. When they entered the university's main gates, one of the headstones "listed fourteen degrees windward and then returned to a normal position," Austgen said. "Some say Gipp had a hand in the waving tombstones."

Austgen also said Gipp is not the only Notre Dame spirit in Washington Hall. Others are said to include Jim Minerva, a student professor who resided there. He liked to entertain students with trumpet renditions of popular tunes of the day.

"Perhaps he is the one who continues to blow the tunes from the other side," Austgen said.

Washington Hall's manager once told Austgen about hearing a thunderous noise late one afternoon.

"He and a housekeeper were the only ones in the building when they heard a thundering thud that shook the building," he said. "He raced from his office on the southeast ground corner to the north side of the third floor. Both felt the building shaking and yet they found the practice stage empty."

One housekeeper has told Austgen she had heard similar noises. She also encountered other strange occurrences.

"(She) said things would fly off the walls," he said. "Things would not just drop, but they would fly 10 feet away from her. She called them generators of energy."

One August night in 2000, the housekeeper told him, things simply went out of control.

"She said 'I walked past the harpsichord and it played a note.' I told it not to start with me today, that I was too busy, and it played the same note again. I jumped all around and I could make it play any more notes," she told him.

Another time, a prop sword fell on the floor while no one else was in the room. A fan blade flew off the fan and barely missed her. She told Austgen she was even poked on the forehead by one of the ghosts. The incident left a red mark on her skin.

Another of the custodians told Austgen of an elderly, balding man with an Irish accent he encountered in the hall. The man asked him to help him open a window. The custodian was concerned; he hadn't seen the fellow in the dorm before, but the man assured him he was associated with the building. Not totally convinced, the custodian turned to open the window, and when he turned back to question the man further, he was gone.

The custodian told Austgen of the experience.

"I told him I thought I might have a solution," Austgen said. "Throughout the years several Holy Cross brothers have died in Washington Hall. I gathered up a few death notices with pictures that I showed him. There were three pictures in all. One was Brother Canute Lardner, an Irish man and a fifty-five year veteran of campus life. He was balding."

Lardner died in February 1946. He died while watching a movie in Washington Hall. Without hesitation, the custodian picked Lardner's picture.

It's all part of the lore at Notre Dame, whether brought about by leprechauns or caused by the spirits of the Potawatomi Indians, who once owned the land on which the university was constructed. Columbus Hall, one of the university's earliest buildings, is said to be haunted by phantom Native Americans who roam the campus on horseback. The phantom riders and their steeds gallop up the hall's front steps.

DePauw University

Books about hauntings are not very rare, but haunted books are another matter entirely.

The books that triggered the discovery of the ghost of former Indiana Gov. James Whitcomb were "The Poems of Ossian, the Son of Fingal," two slender, disintegrating volumes of Indian poetry tied together with a ribbon.

The books had been printed in Scotland and presented to Gov. Whitcomb by Christopher Harrison in 1802. Later, Whitcomb donated the Ossian volumes and others in his rare book collection to the Asbury University with the caveat that the books could not be checked out.

Back around 1900, a student thumbed through the books and found them intriguing. Since the books were for reference only, he decided to slip the small, slim volumes in his pocket so he could read them and return them later.

That night, he awakened to the sight of an apparition looking for the books he'd taken. The terrified student is said to have returned the books to the library bright and early the next morning. In the years since, the ghost was determined to be that of the former governor, who apparently wants to make sure his collection or rare tomes remains intact.

Earlham College

A small Quaker college founded in 1847, Earlham prides itself on a residence project that brings together like-minded individuals from different cultures. In additions to standard dorm life, the college offers themed residence houses for students from specific cultural groups, specific interests, or majors. It also offers friendships houses for students who wish to form communities based on friendship.

One of the residence houses is Wilbur House, which has in recent years been home to students interested in computer science and environmentally conscious living.

The house holds nine students, but there may be a few extra residents who don't take up much space there as well.

Before becoming college property, Wilbur House was a rental property and among the tenants was a group of elderly women suffering from lung cancer. All died in the house and reportedly, their spirits remain there, along with the spirit of a little girl who also died at the home. Her spirit has been observed floating by one of the house's windows.

Iowa

Coe College

Busy on campus during her life, Helen has remained just as busy in death.

Helen Esther Roberts was born December 29, 1899, in Strawberry Point, Iowa. She came to Coe College after graduating from high school in the spring of 1918, and had only been on campus for two weeks before an epidemic of Spanish influenza struck. She contracted the disease and died October 19, 1918, from pneumonia and a cardiac condition caused by the disease weakening the walls of her heart.

"The young woman died as a result of the Spanish flu epidemic," said James Phifer, president of Coe College. "The Spanish flu epidemic happened immediately after World War I ended. It killed more people worldwide than died in the World War. It was a pandemic and was devastating to the population around the globe. And, unfortunately, it took the life of one of our students."

During her short time at Coe, Helen pledged Delta Delta Delta sorority and lived on the second floor of Voorhees Hall. She was transferred to the infirmary on the third floor when she became ill. It was there that she died.

Because her life came to such an abrupt end, it is said that she roams Voorhees Hall and the Coe campus. There are many stories and legends about sightings of her ghost, and strange occurrences on campus have long been attributed to Helen.

The Tri-Delt floor seems to be where most of Helen's activities are reported; her status as a pledge seems to continue her bond with the sorority. The room on the west wing of the second floor where Helen lived is rumored to have a cold wall, a wall on which no objects will remain hanging. It was in the same room where Kate Huck, a 1996 Coe graduate, woke up in the middle of the night and glanced at her Tri-Delt composite portrait that hung next to her bed. There she saw that instead of the faces of her sorority sisters, the face of Helen replaced each one.

Helen's spirit is also said to have taken up residence in an old grandfather clock in Voorhees. The clock had been donated to the school by Helen's family, Phifer said. At night, her ghost has been known to leave the clock and play the piano in the parlor or ascend the stairs and visit her old room. Late at night, an apparition in white sometimes appears at the foot of students' beds. Sometimes it slams doors or pulls off the bedcovers of sleeping students.

It is legend that each year, on the anniversary of Helen's death, she appears and steps from the clock. Students gather around the clock and await her appearance. For many years the clock remained in the main lobby of Voorhees, but eventually began to break with regularity. The clock was moved to Stuart Hall in the 1970s and placed outside the president's office, where attempts were made to repair it. The clock is still there today.

For a while during 2000, a "GhostCam" was installed by Iowa.com just outside the president's office. It allowed students, alumni, and anyone with Internet access the chance to monitor the eighty-two year-old ghost's comings and goings around the clock. Helen proved to be camera shy. There were no official sightings during the period the cameras were in operation.

"We put the HelenCam up as almost a kind of family joke, to see when she came from the clock," Phifer said. " Our PR director wanted to give her a little daylight. She wasn't spotted during that time. She had the good sense to stay out of the way while the camera nosed about her domain and she has not been seen since."

In the eight decades since her death, Helen sightings continue on Coe's campus. Many of the students don't know the facts behind Helen Esther Roberts' death, so stories abound as to why her spirit remains on campus. Some say she searches for a diary she left behind, others believe she simply likes to stir things up. The stories continue and are an important part of Coe College history.

"She is just a quiet member of the family," Phifer said. "She doesn't interfere with the operation of the college at all."

Buena Vista University

Most of us enjoy waking up to the sound of a loved one murmuring softly in our ear. Few things soften the transition from slumber to full consciousness.

Imagine what a jolt it would be, though, if you woke up to the whispers, but you lived alone.

Those sweet nothings are part of the work of a playful poltergeist who lives on the second floor of the Storm Lake university's Pierce Hall. Residents have footsteps running through the empty hallways and have seen silent spirits standing alongside their beds. Items in their rooms get mysteriously moved, lights and appliances seem to turn themselves on and off at will and then there's some wall banging thrown in for good measure.

Iowa State University

Iowa State University's Gold Star Hall in the Memorial Union is home to a lone and lonely female spirit.

Gold Star Hall, a war memorial, is home to a female ghost lonely for a little girl talk. Hers is the only name engraved on the World War I section of the memorial, alongside veterans from World War I and II, the Korean Conflict, and Vietnam.

Dedicated to the memory of ISU students who died in battle, Memorial Union emits a constant, unexplained low moan. The eerie noise is said to be the haunting voice of the lone female graduate of ISU to die in World War I.

"The student union at Iowa State incorporates a memorial to men and women who attended or graduated from Iowa State who perished in the line of duty. We don't really know for sure, but suspect our ghost might be Hortense Elizabeth Wind, the only woman listed in the World War I names in our memorial hall," said Katherine Svec, marketing coordinator for the Iowa State Memorial Union. "She graduated in 1915 and became a Red Cross nurse. We think after all these years with the guys, she's just lonely for another woman to talk to. And then there's that name – Wind."

Hortense is thought to be behind the sounds heard late in the night at the union.

"We have staff in the building twenty-four hours a day," Svec said. "There have been occasional reports from those who work late at night of sounds they couldn't explain – doors closing, the sounds of footsteps, etcetera. Lacking any other explanation, a ghost seemed like a likely culprit."

Whoever it is, the union's spirit seems to be a friendly sort.

"Although the sounds our staff heard were a bit eerie, they were not particularly scary – not something like stalking or preying," Svec said.

She added the story of Hortense is one the staff at Memorial Union – MU – embraces and even perpetuates.

"Students do like the stories – the ghost is one of many associated with the MU. We tell them as often as we can get them to listen."

Obviously, they do.

Once in recent years, Svec said the custodial staff found a piece of paper folded up and tucked behind a radiator vent near the spot where Wind's name is inscribed.

"It was a friendly letter from some women students to Hortense, trying to provide some girl chatter," Svec said. "It was very sweet."

A visit to the student union will not only bring the sounds of Hortense, but the sights, too. Svec said the twelve decorative stained glass windows depict images and symbols throughout the years. One panel honors Hortense with a scene of a nurse on the battlefield.

The Memorial Union is not the only campus location with a ghost. Shattuck Theatre was also said to be haunted. Frederica Shattuck was very involved in theater at ISU. She is said to have haunted the theater bearing her name until it was torn down. She then moved in at Fisher Theater.

Drama students and crew members say they hear voices when no one else is around.

Shattuck's wheelchair was donated to the drama department to use as a prop. It is now said to roll to center stage and face the audience without the assistance of human hands.

At the Farm House Museum, visitors are invited to relax on the porch with a cold glass of lemonade, or warm up in the parlor with hot cider. The Farm House Museum is at once a historic place and a comfortable, welcoming place as well.

The three-story, fourteen-room building was the first structure on ISU's campus, and a pair of sisters whose family lived fifty years in the house are said to live on there still. They're credited with pulling pranks such as locking the doors from the inside, turning on the lights, and throwing open the windows after staff carefully shuts them.

Close all the parlor doors at Freeman Hall and the huffy ghost of its namesake, Alice Freeman, will open them. Birch-Welch-Roberts Hall and Linden Hall also have been the site of ghostly activity.

University of Northern Iowa

Here's a university that has ghosts from A to Z. That's Augie, of Lawther Hall, to Zelda, of the Strayer-Wood Theatre.

Augie's home, Lawther Hall, was originally called the Bartlett Hall Addition, and construction on it began in 1939. It cost $400,000 and housed 300 women in their junior and senior years at the college. In 1940, it was given its current name, in honor of Anna B. Lawther, a leader of the suffrage movement in Iowa.

In the mid-seventies, dorm residents started noticing their personal items were disappearing and strange footsteps were heard in the attic.

One night, a resident reported a male visitor in a pin-striped suit walking unattended in the hall. The residence assistant called security and several people discreetly followed the man upstairs toward the attic. He removed a set of keys, opened the attic door and went inside. When security arrived, they found no trace of the snappily dressed visitor.

Up through the late 1990s, residents happily gave tours of Augie's Attic.

Zelda seems to enjoy timing her visits to Strayer-Wood Theatre well, waiting until only a handful of people remain. Then she opens up with a barrage of strange noises and screams. She's even been known to dis the remaining audience.

Wartburg College

In some of the rooms at Ernst House in The Manors – most eerily, No.13 – residents have noticed doors swing open and close on their own, even when the windows are shut. They say they understand the place is haunted, by they don't know by whom or why, and they're not particularly intrigued about it.

Kansas

Kansas State University

With all the Greek ghosts roaming the picturesque Manhattan campus, perhaps the university should consider a Panhellenic Apparition Council.

One of the university's better-known ghosts is Duncan, who haunts the old Theta Xi house, now the home to Pi Kappa Phi. Duncan suffered a freak injury during initiation – he was accidentally hit on the head with a paddle. The blow caused a concussion and the resulting swelling and damage to his brain was fatal.

When Phi Gamma Delta opened its Chi Deuteron chapter in 1968, the members did some sprucing up and removed a set of Theta Xi paddles hanging from the library wall. They found reddish-brown spots under one, and no matter how much they painted, nor how dark the paint, the stain always showed through. They resorted to paneling the area. Finally, after the Fijis moved to a new home on Hunting Street in 1993, the house became home to the Pi Kapps, who decided the wall again needed remodeling to hide the marks.

Duncan, for the most part, is harmless, but sometimes his little pranks make him a pest. His door slamming, fiddling with light switches, and other childish pranks make the residents testy. Others have reported seeing Duncan, staring blankly, roaming the campus.

Another house boasts of a pair of ghosts from the building's former use.

"The Delta Sigma Phi fraternity house used to be a hospital," said Dana Slaughter Rati, who studied biology and education at K-State from 1992 to 1997 and like many K-Staters, learned early on about her ghostly classmates. "It is haunted by a former patient and a nurse."

The nurse has been diligent through the years. She's been observed from time to time, she has been observed making her rounds, ministering to her patients.

George is believed to be the ghost of an elderly patient who loved to watch *Star Trek*. He died when he fell from his bed and suffocated. His body was found the next day. George is a bit of a troublemaker, but in a playful way. He's been known to stir things up on the third floor by moving items and furniture, hiding things and occasionally throwing things around.

But that's not all of the Greek ghosts.

"The Lambda Chi house and Chi Omega are haunted by former member," Rati said. A sophomore who hanged himself in a file room still appears as a white haze at the Kappa Sigma house, wafting along the stairway, second floor and along the roof.

K-State's best-known ghost wasn't part if the Greek scene. It is believed he was an ill-fated independent named Nick.

The widely held legend is that during the 1950s, Nick was a football player for the Wildcats, and as he dressed for his final game, he did so with anticipation because his family was coming to see him play. He suffered an injury during the game and was taken to an adjacent dormitory kitchen and cafeteria under the bleachers, which was converted to a training room for home games at old Memorial Stadium.

Nick's injuries were more serious than originally thought. His condition deteriorated rapidly and he died on the scene. His parents were killed in an automobile crash on the way to the stadium.

The old kitchen and cafeteria was converted to the Purple Masque Theatre, and except when he's wandering the stadium, looking for his folks, that's where Nick spends his days and nights.

"He now pulls the requisite ghostly pranks in the theater," Rati said. Nick's a no-holds-barred trickster. He's been credited with making fire extinguishers squirt, turns over buckets of paint and generally makes a pest of himself.

If Nick's story seems too otherworldly to be true, apparently it is. Student journalists from the *Kansas State Collegian* checked out the story at the university archives and learned the university has never experienced a football fatality and there was no record of a dormitory kitchen/cafeteria under the bleachers. Which leaves one question: Who's been pulling all those pranks?

Kentucky

Western Kentucky University

Spread out Western Kentucky University's map, close your eyes and touch a spot on it. If one of the school's fifty-three buildings are beneath your fingertip, there's a good chance it has a haunting legend to attached to it.

Haunted legends are big in Kentucky and at WKU in particular. Spirits rate very high there. The university's motto is "The spirit makes the master" and should you spend any time talking with a student, faculty member or staff member, you'll likely get a lesson in "Western spirit." It's that kind of place.

So follow along on your map for this ghostly travelogue of WKU.

Van Meter Hall's ghost tales center around the building's 2,000-seat auditorium, used as a venue for lectures, concerts, plays, commencement and other auspicious occasions. Sometime during 1909 and 1911 as the building was being constructed, a construction worker on the roof spotted an airplane – still quite a curiosity in those days. The momentary distraction caused him to lose his equilibrium and he fell to his death on the stage below.

The worker's fall left a large blood stain, which resisted attempts to expunge and even today, people say, a reddish glow radiated from the stage at the point where the man hit the ground and he lives on in the auditorium today.

Lynn Niedermeier, an archival assistant at WKU, said the story of the red glow of Van Meter Hall is her favorite story among those she has researched in her five years there.

"We do have a good bank of legends," she says. "In University Archives, we keep vertical files on any subject relating to the university. One is on ghosts and ghost stories. We have clippings from the campus newspaper, the local newspaper, the yearbook and every year at Halloween, someone wants our research. We also have a fairly good collection of folklife archives with oral interviews."

Niedermeier has investigated the story of the ill-fated workman and has attempted to prove and disprove the tale.

"One student was in his dressing room after a performance," she said. "He was taking off his makeup while looking in the mirror. He saw a face in the mirror and he assumed it was the ghost."

The ghost also has been known to appear as a blue light.

Described by those who saw they've seen him as a man in his fifties dressed in white, the ghost's activities include fiddling with the light switches and curtains and re-arranging furniture and music stands. Staff members from the University Relations department who moved into Van Meter in 1997, arrived at work one morning to find a large table had been repositioned across the lobby. They also have experienced weird computer glitches that they attribute to the ghost's fascination with modern technology.

Potter Hall, a women's dormitory constructed in 1921, is said to be haunted by a young woman who committed suicide there. Known as Allison or derisively as Casparella, she was said to remain a presence in the hall, tramping along the halls, dropping coins into the vending machines, turning switches on and off, moving furniture and opening and closing doors. Residents said they'd hear their names called out in the hall, but would see no one. Additionally, residents were troubled by cold breezes that would occasionally circulate in closed rooms.

Potter Hall has been transformed into an administration building and in recent years, Allison seems to have slowed, but a 1994 incident when strange banging was reported coming from the room in which she allegedly died suggests otherwise.

Niedermeier said Allison's legend also is widely known on campus. Students learn the story when they arrive as freshmen and over the years, add their own spin.

"This ghost is a prankster," she said. "Turning lights off, moving things around. One RA had the life scared out of her when she heard a terrible banging on the pipes from the basement area. It sounded as if (Allison) was banging on the pipes."

Other reportedly haunted buildings include:

• Schneider Hall, where the restless spirit of an ax-murder victim returns each spring to avenge her death.

• Rodes-Harlin Hall, where a suicide victim returns to tap on her former dorm neighbors' doors, but scampers away before they answer.

• Pearce-Ford Hall, where a dead elevator repairman pushes all the buttons during the summer months.

• Kentucky Building, home to the library's Special Collections department and a repository of historical materials relating to Kentucky and its citizens. Eerie sounds and chilling puffs of air greet some who come to visit

• McLean Hall, named in honor of Mattie McLean, the secretary who served the university's first two presidents, Henry Hardin Cherry and Paul Garrett. After her death in 1954, her friendly, motherly spirit is said to have moved in at the hall that bore her name.

• Barnes-Campbell Hall, supposedly haunted by the ghost of an RA who was crushed as he attempted to fix a stuck elevator car. The RA, who had just stepped out of the showers when he was summoned to fix the elevator, is said to leave watery footprints on the floor.

Louisiana

Loyola University New Orleans

Do you see dead people? The Big Easy is easily one of America's most haunted cities, and Loyola has a few haunts to call its own.

At Marquette Hall, the university's signature building, there's said to be a parade of spirits. The fifth floor of the university's oldest building formerly was the site of the anatomy laboratories and some folks say some of those who – willingly or not – lent their bodies to science have stayed on. The building is now used as the university's administrative headquarters, with the president's office, bursar's and financial aid offices, admissions, and other departments.

Greenville Hall and the old library buildings also are said to be haunted.

Maine

University of Maine at Farmington

Throughout her legendary career, Lillian Nordica's critics constantly gushed over her seemingly effortless performances. She seemed so natural, so at home on the stage, they marveled.

They were wrong, of course. Nordica's seemingly effortless performances were achieved as the result of her relentless pursuit for perfection, evidenced by long, arduous practices. But it was true that she was at home on the stage. In many ways, the stage was her refuge from life.

Nordica, born Lillian Bayard Norton in Farmington in 1857, came from a family that believed in strict religious values and hard work. For enjoyment, they turned to music. By age 6, Lillian's talent had been recognized and the family moved to Boston so she could attend classes at the New England Conservatory of Music.

She grew into "The Yankee Diva," a lovely, statuesque woman with thick chestnut hair and expressive dark eyes. She adopted the stage name of "Giglio Nordica," literally "Lily of the Northland," to make her more appealing to Italian audiences. Over time, she was widely known as La Nordica.

Nordica possessed a voice of power, range and beauty, and thanks to her grueling practices, foreign audiences marveled that she sang her roles in accentless German or Italian.

Whether abroad or in the United States, Nordica, nearly always clad in her trademark pearls, was warmly embraced by audiences. She achieved commercial success and artistic acclaim, but her personal life was less appealing. She entered into three loveless marriages all of which failed and failed to provide her what she wanted most from life – a child.

By her late 50s, her voice had lost its intensity, range and majesty and Nordica embarked on a final world tour. Her ship ran aground in the shallows of the Gulf of Papua in December 1913. The boat was emptied to try and lighten its load and move it from the shallows, but Nordica caught pneumonia in the harsh conditions. She was taken to a hospital in Batavia, Java, where she died in May 1914.

The University of Maine at Farmington recognizes their native daughter's contributions with the Nordica Auditorium in the university's Merrill Hall, a multi-purpose building that also houses the president's office.

People have reported hearing the disembodied sound of a soprano's voice late at night when the auditorium's lights are out and the building is otherwise empty. Others have said they feel a distinctive presence in the building, a presence that urges them to break out in song. Perhaps it is La Nordica herself, they suggest, at home forever on a stage named in her honor.

Maryland

Towson University

Auburn House, a stunning example of Italianate Federal architecture, was named in honor of Oliver Goldsmith's 1770 poem. The home was built in 1790 by Captain Charles Ridgely as a dowager house for his wife, Rebecca Dorsey.

Rebecca lived at the mansion from 1791 until her death in 1812. During those years, some of the best and brightest names in the fledgling nation passed between the sentinel elm trees dubbed "Bride & Groom" and partied there, including George Washington.

After Rebecca Dorsey's death, the home had several owners until Henry Chrystie Turnbull acquired it in 1836. He added a barn and formal gardens, but in 1949, a severe storm rumbled through the area. During the storm, the mansion caught fire and destroyed the old home. Turnbull rebuilt it on its original foundation the next year, using the original parts, whenever possible. Despite Trumbull's loving restoration and improvements and enlargements made by subsequent owners, the home never was the same after the fire.

"During the 1849 fire, a young woman named Martha lost her life," said Towson University archivist Nancy Gonce.

Martha's relationship to the Turnbull family was unclear. She might have been a servant, nanny, teacher or tutor to the children or a mistress to Henry Turnbull. Some theorize Ann Turnbull, Henry's wife, murdered Martha, using the storm and fire as a diversion.

"It is rumored that her spirit still moves through the rooms today," Gonce said. "Staff working in Auburn have reported pages of books turning, desks mysteriously locking, unexplained relocation of items in work areas, windows being opened on the upper floors."

Auburn House became the property of Towson University in 1975, the same year the building was placed on the National Register of Historic Places.

Auburn House is home to the athletic department's offices, the Auburn Society, the Institute for Learning in Retirement and the Center for Economic Education in Maryland and also serves as a venue for university and private events.

The Bride and Groom elms died eventually, but Auburn House's longtime spirit resident still calls it home.

Community College of Baltimore County

Officially it's the Administration Building, or the A Building, but everyone on CCBC's Catonsville campus calls it The Mansion. The 130-acre Hilton family estate provides a gracious, spacious home for the college's administrative and business offices, and to the apparition of a woman in a nightgown, who walks the halls with her candle.

The building also is reported to be the home of some poltergeist activity, but it's said to be as refined and dignified as the antebellum building.

Massachusetts

Smith College

Sessions House, built in 1751, is a family house converted for use as a residence hall. The house's original owners were the Jonathan Hunt family, and legend holds that their daughter Lucy found a secret meeting place in a hidden stairway in the house so she could be close with her lover, General Burgoyne. Like many such clandestine relationships, this one was doomed, and by the 1880s, the ghost of the brokenhearted general was said to haunt the staircase.

Over the years, the gender of the ghost has changed and it is now Lucy who is claimed to inhabit the home, the oldest residence facility on campus. As an homage to Lucy, a tradition began at the college for residents of the home to look for the secret passageway at Halloween each year. Those who found it received an award. Outsiders believed that the exercise was sham, little more than an excuse to throw a Halloween party, that no such passageway existed.

In 1996, staff from the college's physical plant examined the house's structure during renovations and discovered a secret passageway of sorts does really exist.

The project director noted in his report: "The photos and drawings show that the size of the voids was large enough to fit into and although we found no concrete evidence of a stair or tunnel, the possibility certainly exists."

Boston University

The ghost of playwright Eugene O'Neill lives a peaceful, quiet existence in Suite 401 of Shelton Hall, where he died November 27, 1953.

The building at the time was operating as the Hotel Shelton. The usual manifestations are persistent phantom door and wall knocking, window shades that roll up without prompting, conversations heard in the empty hallway, and flickering of lights in the room. Twice in 1994, an apparition was reported dashing into the two-bedroom suite.

The ghost of Henry Jewett, an Australian actor and director, is blamed for the disappearance or alteration of students' work at the Boston University Theatre, formerly the Jewett Repertory Theatre. Jewett reportedly has made a few personal appearances, dressed in Elizabethan garb.

Massachusetts College of Liberal Arts

Residents in B8 at the Berkshire Towers usually just shrug it off when they open their doors after a knock and find the hallway empty. Just another prank of a never-seen but often-heard female ghost who hangs out there, they say. It's not uncommon to hear footsteps, a rattle of keys or someone fiddling with the doorknob before the distinctive knock.

Stonehill College

On the morning of November 6, 1932, Frederick Lothrop "Freddie" Ames Jr., twenty-seven, and two more of his highfalutin society friends left Ames' fifty room palatial family home on Stone House Hill in Easton after a night of partying. They flew in Ames' Cessna Cabin monoplane to East Boston. Then Ames, heiress Frances Burnett, twenty-two, banker/executive Frank Penrose Sproule, twenty-five, and Salud, Ames' wire-haired Mexican terrier, climbed back for the return flight to Stone House Hill before going on to Newport.

They never reached their destination.

Rich, bright, and an accomplished pilot, Ames threw care to the wind as he pulled back the throttle. A Harvard dropout, he looked the part of the flying ace with his brilliantined black hair and jaunty mustache. Whether behind the wheel of a racing car, a yacht, or in the cockpit, he was a daredevil, and that day was no different. He did a few stunts, spins, and some loops, but in the final one, something went very wrong. He couldn't pull the plane out and it crashed in a field in the Tower Hill section of nearby Randolph. All aboard died. When rescuers reached the crash site, they saw a curious bluish mist above it.

From the moment the nose of the plane burrowed into the field, rumors began and many persist to this day, including those about the Ames family's ghostly pursuits. Rumors of the ghost of Mary Callender Ames, Freddie's younger sister, already have been proven untrue. Unfounded tales of Freddie's decapitation in the crash, the site of the crash and his burial spot also were dispelled. Ames' ashes were buried in the family's plot behind Unity Church in Easton.

But Freddie Ames lives on at Stone House Hill, many insist. Only one student has claimed to see Freddie Ames' ghost, but many have seen the distinctive blue mist that rises over the college's pond now and again.

The Stone House Hill home is now Donahue Hall, part of Stonehill College, which was given to the Holy Cross Fathers in 1936. Students insist that the blue mist that swirls through the campus is simply Freddie, always the stunt flier, even in the spirit realm.

Michigan

Michigan State University

The ghost of a young man named Bill haunts the Wharton Center for the Performing Arts in Lansing. Killed in the early 1980s in a violent beating, the young man has not yet taken his final curtain call in the campus theater.

David Lower, then a student usher, ran into Bill unexpectedly late one evening in 1989. Working late on a project in the theater with student house manager Chris Buck, Lower borrowed Buck's keys and went in search of a restroom on the floor which housed all the performers' dressing rooms.

"I opened a door with Chris's key about a third of the way," Lower remembered. "There was a guy in a white button-down shirt and black chinos sitting in a director's chair facing a lit theatre mirror. He was in profile to me. I was so shocked to see him there, I opened the door all the way. At that sound, the man turned and half-faced me. I immediately apologized to him and closed the door because I did not want to disturb him."

However, Lower knew only he and his best friend Buck were in the building. They had locked the theater together earlier in the evening and no one else had entered since. So he used the key again to open the door. There was no one in the chair. Upon a further search, Lower found no one was hiding anywhere in the room or the adjoining bathroom. There was simply no other living being on the same floor with Lower.

Months later, Buck and Lower, who were also roommates, discussed the events of that evening for the first time. After Lower had finished telling his story, Buck pulled a framed photo from the bottom drawer of his desk.

"Was this the guy?" Buck asked.

"Yeah, that's him," Lower said, almost in disbelief. "Who is that?"

Buck told Lower that was Bill, a ghostly presence in the building. Buck had heard all the stories that had been passed along by the student employees and soon after he was hired onto the staff at the Wharton Center, he decided to make his peace with Bill. He simply sat in the theater late one evening and introduced himself, saying he was there to do a job and would neither bother Bill nor invade his space in the theater. After that one-sided discussion, Buck said he always felt he had a guardian angel while working at the Wharton Center and indeed credits Bill with his rapid rise through the ranks of student management.

Lower and Buck surmised that because they were roommates and often shared clothing, Bill had made his presence known to Lower simply because he thought he was his "friend" Buck. After all, Lower was wearing Buck's sweatshirt and was carrying his keys.

Officials at MSU said there have been no official reports of ghosts or otherworldly activities in the Wharton Center — just stories that students tell to scare one another. Students talk about objects moving from place to place, doors opening and closing by themselves, noises heard late at night and lights turning on and off with no one in the room. Buck and Lower think differently.

Central Michigan University

Of all the buildings on campus, Warriner Hall seems most appropriate for a ghost to call home. Built in 1928 as a home for the college's administration building and library, Warriner's Gothic lines are softened a bit by the ivy that climbs the wall, but the building is imposing nonetheless.

In 1937, a cafeteria worker named Theresa Schumacher died of a broken neck in a freak elevator accident in the building. Over the years, odd things happened in the hall, with lights flashing on and off and the sounds of footsteps in the main stairway. In rooms 503 and 504, pounding sounds were clearly audible. In 1969, students saw Theresa on the fifth floor of the tower. She's been seen occasionally ever since.

Eastern Michigan University

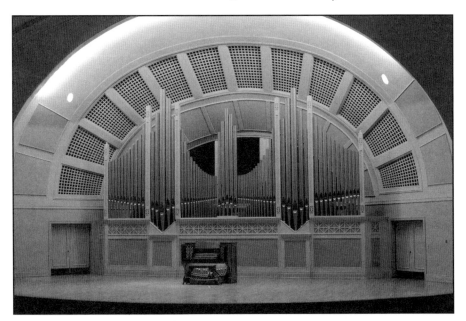

Pease Auditorium, built in 1915, seats 1,500 and is the home of the university's famed pipe organ and one decidedly unfriendly spirit.

Walking into the darkness of Pease from the bright Michigan sunlight, one can easily imagine it as home to some sort of otherworldly being. The omnipresent pipe organ, ornate glasswork in the ceiling, hand-tooled wooden moldings and architecture from another era make Pease the perfect setting for a ghostly encounter. With no one else in the building late at night, things that go bump in the night would terrify even the bravest of visitors.

Rumors abound on the Ypsilanti university's 800-acre campus about the ghost of Pease. Music majors who practice long hours in the stately building swear the ghost of Frederick Pease, the building's namesake, roams the catwalks, the hallways, the dressing rooms and stage looking for opportunities to frighten anyone who dares trespass in his building.

"Any music major who has ever graduated or taken classes at EMU can tell you stories about the ghost of Pease," says music department head David Woike.

But is the ghost fact or fiction?

In 1980, now-legendary newspaper designer Tim Harrower was then the enterprising editor of the university's student newspaper, the *Eastern Echo*. He wrote a piece of historical fiction in the school's humor magazine, *Spectrum*. His epic saga about the ghost of Pease, rife with intentional inaccuracies, set ablaze the rumor of an unearthly entity in the historic theater. After publication, several students stepped forward, declaring they had encountered the angry specter of Frederick Pease.

Rita Abent, then the college's publication adviser, said "Tim wrote the piece with deliberate errors of fact – such as listing F. Walter Briggs as university president. F. Walter Briggs was never university president. It was a work of fiction that was so well-written, it took on a life of its own."

Abent said the piece was written with enough factual historical data that it made people wonder. Some were convinced there was a ghost in Pease. Some were upset they had been duped. Others fell somewhere in the middle. And some, like Abent, celebrated it for the excellent piece of writing it was.

"People read it and could then add what they knew to the story," she said. "Even though the story didn't exist before, they were able to say 'Yeah, and then here is what happened.' Or they could say 'That's not what I heard at all.' And then tie it to other legends involving other campus landmarks. That certainly helps a legend grow."

Opposing page:
The famed pipe organ at Pease Auditorium at Eastern Michigan University.

Mary Ida Yost, Harrower's theory teacher and retired university organist, spent many, many hours in Pease Auditorium, both alone and with students.

"I could tell you a lot of harrowing stories about teaching in Pease," she said one summer evening. "But they all involve real people."

The auditorium is located on the outer edge of the campus to make it accessible to the paying public, and is also close to the Ypsilanti community and its residents. Some of those residents live in local halfway houses. Some used to often turn up at Pease at inopportune times. Yost recalls having some of them escorted out by the campus police after interrupting her teaching.

"I've never seen anything in Pease," said David Lower, a former Pease building manager. "Once you start hearing things, you start looking for things. We did and they still do keep a ghost light on. The only time you turn the lights off is when the building is empty. We did it at Pease – most major theaters do it."

Is the story true? It depends on whom you ask. University officials say there is no ghost in Pease Auditorium. Students who spend a majority of their time there say there is.

As for Abent?

"I think there are ghosts in every building," she said. "We just happened to have an excellent creative writer who captured the essence of this one."

Northern Michigan University

Perry Fezatt came to the university after serving as a paratrooper in the U.S. Army during World War II. As a thirty-year employee, he knew everyone at the school and they all liked him. And why not? Fezatt was a short, stocky man with a well-developed sense of humor and a taste for practical jokes. His warm, friendly nature made friends for him easily.

He served the university as custodian at Forrest Roberts Theatre, which was called The Little Theatre when it opened in 1963. Anyone who needed him to help loosen a sticky lock, move tables and chairs or clean up a spill only had to listen for him. He almost always whistled while he worked.

Despite his warmth and good humor, Fezatt had hit some major potholes on his journey through life. His wife died young and he never remarried. By the time he had reached his late fifties, he found himself as the caregiver to his elderly mother, with whom he lived. To make matters worse, he learned he suffered from heart problems himself. Still, he looked ahead to retirement, when he'd be free from caring from his mother and able to move to the southern part of the Upper Peninsula.

He never got to realize that dream. He suffered a heart seizure and died while working in the theater's elevator.

Since his death, people who work in the theater have noted it seems at times as though he'd never left. Some folks say they've sensed his presence throughout the building. Others say they've heard his familiar whistle.

The most interesting manifestations have been in the elevator, which seems to have inherited Fezatt's penchant for practical jokes. Riders who push the "up" button find themselves traveling down. Another rider stepped into the elevator, pushed the button, felt the little jerk when it begins moving, but when the doors opened, found he was at the same floor he'd left.

Minnesota

St. Olaf College

Ghosts have been an accepted part of campus life for over 100 years. In the first edition of the college newspaper, *The Manitou Messenger*, in 1887, it was noted "two ghosts were seen parading the upper floor at Ladies Hall Friday evening."

The site of many unexplained events was Ytterboe Hall, which has since been replaced with a new facility bearing the same name.

The land on which the original hall, built in 1900 and called the Boys Dormitory, was built was considered sacred by local Indians.

In 1903, a scarlet fever epidemic swept the campus and Halvor T. Ytterboe, a professor and head hall resident for the boys dormitory embarked on an effort to disinfect the hall, scrubbing all exposed surfaces with formaldehyde. Tragically, he was unaware of the toxic effects of the solution and eventually died as a result of exposure to it. He was forty-six.

In 1915, the hall was named in his honor. Over the years, a variety of mild poltergeist effects have been reported. Dorm dwellers reported they felt as though they've been brushed by unseen others walking past them.

Sometime during the 1970s, a student was startled and quickly annoyed by the sound of forties-style big-band dance music blaring near her. Quickly, she rummaged around her room and found the radio that was the source of the noise, but was shocked to discover it was unplugged.

A female student living in Thorson Hall was jolted from a sound sleep by the sound of a screaming child in her midst. She was dumfounded, to say the least. The room had been locked and the hall was not the place where lost children showed up in the middle of the night. Furthermore, her roommate slept soundly throughout the few minutes the child screamed, then turned and disappeared.

When the other women in the hall woke the next morning, she asked those living near her room if they had heard anything. None had.

St. Mary's University

The confluence of several violent events over the years seems to have resulted in the presence of a resentful spirit at this lovely Catholic university.

Those events include the attempted assassination of a bishop by a priest in the school's chapel, the trial and commitment of the assailant, and the electrocution death of a third priest.

Bishop Patrick Heffron and Father Laurence Michael Lesches had known each other for many years and never truly saw eye-to-eye. Heffron felt uneasy around Lesches and questioned his ability as a priest. Lesches accused Heffron of keeping him from his dream of becoming pastor of his own parish. Heffron was celebrating Mass one August morning in 1915 when he saw a figure dart into the chapel. In short order he heard three loud pops and felt pain. One of the bullets had missed its mark, but one hit him in the thigh and another pierced a lung. The bishop survived, Lesches was apprehended and sent to trial, where he was found not guilty by reason of insanity. He was committed to an asylum and lived out his days there.

Even from the asylum, Lesches' presence continued to be felt on St. Mary's campus.

In May 1931, the charred remains of Father Edward Lynch, another rival of Lesches, were found at college when a nun entered his room to clean it. She found his body sprawled across the bed, forming a human cross. The body was facing up and was badly burned. The priest's Bible was charred, but nothing else in the room caught on fire — not even the bed sheets. The cause of his death was a mystery, and although Lesches was still confined, many believed the priest was somehow responsible. Lynch had been a close friend of Bishop Heffron and therefore and enemy of Father Lesches. The two had lived together in Saint Mary's Hall and had often argued.

Lesches often quoted the Bible and had once repeated to Lynch the passage, "And the Lord shall come again in the sounding of trumpets." When the charred remains of Lynch's Bible were closely studied, the only readable passage was: "And the Lord shall come again to the sounding of trumpets."

Lynch's death was officially attributed to accidental electrocution, but no one has been able to explain it, or the strange occurrences that have taken place on the third floor of Heffron since Lesches' death

Shortly after the eighty-four year-old priest's death, students on the third floor of Heffron Hall reported a tapping sound up and down the hall at odd hours of the night. In life, Lesches had walked with a gold-handled black cane.

Additionally, sudden cold spots can be felt in different places on the third floor.

University of Minnesota

Times are quieter at Nicholson Hall in Minneapolis these days. The rugged brick and stone building with the Romanesque arched entryway once was a hub of activity as the campus' student union and bookstore, but now it's home to the university's college of architecture and landscape architecture.

Things heated up in 1996 when an angry poltergeist making a one-night stand threw a phone book at a campus security officer and caused his two-way radio to sputter out as he made his rounds.

Also on the Twin Cities Campus, howling noises have been reported many times at the Walter Library.

Mississippi

Mississippi State University

Mississippi State University is one of the few institutions of higher education in America that seems not to have a ghost legend or two haunting its campus. The university has, however, had two tragedies happen that left students there at the time feeling distinctly haunted.

The first is the Old Main. By anyone's account, Old Main was quite a dormitory. By its size alone, it became the kind of place legends are made of. Its corridors were so long, students occasionally drove motorcycles down them. Children rollerskated in them.

In 1959, a fire destroyed the grand old hall. It was seventy-nine years old when it went up in flames, and during those years, more than 40,000 young men called it home. It had been built in sections, with the first portion completed in 1879 or 1880. Today, McCool Hall and the University Union stand in Old Main's place.

Fire had been a frequent but unwanted guest in the dormitory. Students seemed to be constantly playing pranks that got out of control. No one who ever threw a firecracker across the hall or started a garbage can blaze ever thought it could bring the old dorm down, but it did.

The fateful January night of the blaze had been normal in most respects. In the middle of the night in exam week and many of the 9000 students were still up, studying. Others had turned in early, hoping a good night's sleep would give them a clear head the next morning. Few paid attention the first calls of "Fire! Fire!" because of all the prank fires that had been set. But this fire was the real thing and it spread with lightning quickness. The building went up quickly and firefighters could do little.

Amazingly, the fire took but one victim, Henry Allen Williamson, who ran back into the dorm to snatch some of his audio equipment

Missouri

Stephens College

A broken heart, not school pride, is what keeps Sarah June Wheeler her at her old alma mater.

Wheeler's ghost remains at Senior Hall at what was once the Baptist Female College. One night, while her roommates were at dinner, Wheeler, who had felt a bit under the weather, lay in her bed. She heard a soft rap on the door and when she opened it, was surprised to see an escaped Confederate soldier, Isaac Johnson, bleeding in her doorway. Taking pity on him, she led him up to her third-floor room and hid him in her closet. She nursed his injuries, fed him and cared for him as best she could under the circumstances. Eventually over the weeks of her caring for him, her feelings turned from concern to love. She took all precautions she could to prevent detection, but somewhere slipped up. The administration learned of him and turned him in to the Union authorities, who made a grisly but visual lesson of him. Three days later, they carried out the sentence against him: Death by firing squad. The execution took place in front of Senior Hall. Moments after the sentence had been carried out, Sarah joined him in death. Stories vary on how she killed herself, either by jumping from the college's bell tower or by plunging down a staircase.

"I think students identify with the story being that it is a she and she is close to their age, if not younger, and that she fell in love holds appeal," says Dr. Alan Havig, who has been teaching American History at Stephens for the past thirty-five years. He said he first heard the tale not long after he arrived in Columbia.

"Every year, by the time I get students in late August or early September, they have already heard the story," Havig said. "Sometimes it's during our lively orientation program. It is passed along. It's a warm and fuzzy story and it puts a personal tint on our traditions."

Havig is not content to let the story become an urban legend. Instead he puts it into context of American History, asking his students what they have heard, then presenting them with the facts. He tells them of a Missouri that was ripped asunder by the Civil War. Neighbors were gunned down in the street. Family members were arrested on the sidewalks. It was a state under siege.

"Missouri was a war zone," Havig said. "There was dying; there was sacrifice; there was pain."

Those who have seen the apparitions have told Havig they see unusual lights or shadows, or catch a glimpse of someone out of the corner of an eye. Some enterprising students used the ten years the building was closed to do some empirical experimentation of their own. When the building, the oldest on campus, was closed for a decade during parts of the seventies and eighties, they'd climb in through a window and hunker in, waiting to see the ghosts.

Renovations at Senior Hall, the oldest building on campus, have increased the spirited activity, and students say Sarah is sure to make an appearance in the bell tower every Halloween at midnight.

Havig said students have told him of other apparitions on campus, too.

"In one of the newer residence halls," he said, "they talk about having seen someone who appears sitting on top of a washing machine or dryer and when they student looks away then looks back, the someone is gone."

Northwest Missouri State University

Roberta Steel was a lovely young woman with a moon face that framed a demure smile. Deep down, beneath her demure exterior, was the heart of a fighter. She had to be to hang on for six months after suffering terrible injuries when a propane take exploded outside her residence hall in April 1951. The blast left twenty-one students injured, and five of them – including Roberta – were seriously injured. Roberta suffered serious burns and went into shock, but held on before succumbing at the end of November. She was the blast's only fatality.

In the years since then, students have seen the hazy silhouette of a woman appear and disappear in what is now Roberta Hall. Residents' keys have a way of appearing and disappearing there and strange noises are heard.

Among other places on campus reported to be haunted include Hudson Hall, where poltergeist activity has been reported in a fourth-floor room. Lillian is the name given to the spirit who resident at the Delta Chi house. Visitors to the basement have reported hearing the disembodied voice of a small girl there.

St. Louis University

University employees are said to be afraid to go into rooms in DuBourg Hall for reasons other than the smell of unwashed socks.

Montana

University of Montana

Jeanette Rankin, who had a special interest in world peace, social issues and women's rights, in 1916 became the first woman elected to the U.S. House of Representatives. She's believed to remain active in the dormitory that bears her name. A public servant has to keep touch with her constituents, which would explain the sound of footsteps when the dorm is empty, and perhaps even the sound of doors closing.

Sometimes serving the constituents means spreading a little lagniappe here and there, too. Legend has it that visitors who enter Rankin Hall and brush off the congresswoman's portrait, greet her and make a little small talk will be rewarded with a present in a nearby trash can.

Other halls with haunted legends on campus include:

• Brantly Hall, home of a phantom German shepherd poking around the building.

• Main Hall, where a dark-haired woman appeared to a custodian as he worked in a rest room, and quickly vanished.

Carroll College

At dead center, if you'll excuse the pun, of Carroll's campus is St. Charles Hall, a stately, imposing edifice that dominates the layout. Built in 1909 of red and white Montana porphyry, it is Carroll's oldest and largest building and serves many purposes, as a residence hall, chapel, visual arts studio, faculty offices, mailroom, and also has classrooms. If one went looking on the campus for the most likely spot for ghosts and ghostly occurrences, they'd go no further. Step behind the battlements and pay a visit. The building is five floors high and packed with stories.

The best-known story is of a well-liked student who died as the result of head injuries suffered when he fell in the rest room and struck his head on a sink. He's credited with roaming the hall and knocking on doors. Campus scuttlebutt persisted that a bloodstain lingered on the sink where the student hit his head and resisted attempts the clean it off. Further examination revealed the "stain" was nothing more than red paint.

Nebraska

Nebraska University

When she was a little girl, Jessica Kennedy loved ghost tales.

"My best friend and I used to sit in the closet with a flashlight and tell each other ghost stories until one of us ran out screaming," she says.

When she followed her mom's footsteps to Nebraska University, her interest in ghost stories picked up again with a project for class. She's kept up with it since then has led students on ghost tours around the campus during the autumn. Among the most interesting sites are her old dorm Neihardt Hall and The Temple, but there are plenty of stories and sites.

"There's so many stories, almost too many," she says. "It really makes you wonder."

Neihardt Hall is the oldest residence hall on the Lincoln campus.

"Neihardt has always been a residence hall," she says. "It was originally Raymond Hall. One of the things I'd heard was it was a hospital with a morgue, but it wasn't."

But that didn't help explain the coffin a maintenance director found in the basement when he arrived at the hall.

"It wasn't some flimsy prop casket," Kennedy said. "It was a real casket, lined."

After lots of searching, the maintenance man donated it to a local funeral home.

When she lived at Neihardt, Kennedy said she found her stereo acted strangely, such as turning itself on by itself.

"I always thought it was just someone messing around with me," she said. On one of her ghost tours, two students pulled her aside and asked her what room she had lived in. She told them and they nodded grimly; they were the room's current residents.

"They had had unexplained and creepy experiences in that same room," she said.

When a cable installer came to Neihardt, he encountered Sara, the ghost of a student who died in an influenza epidemic many years before.

"He turned around and there was a young woman standing there," Kennedy said. "He then realized he could see the door frame through her."

"He left the building very quickly and refused to return," she said.

The Temple Building, more commonly simply called The Temple, was built in 1905 and is "a sort of smaller performing arts building," Kennedy said. "It has a lot of stories."

Many of those stories involve Dallas Williams, a beloved drama professor who was the driving force behind The Temple's success. Williams had a special seat in the back of the theater from where he watched the student thespians. He died of a massive stroke in 1971.

"They always save his seat for him," Kennedy said. "People say they can see his crew cut back there while they're performing."

Once, a local television reporter was preparing to film a segment in The Temple. He'd set up his camera and was waiting for his interview to arrive. He heard the door open and close and then heard footsteps. He turned on his camera and looked through the viewfinder. Nothing.

He looked up.

Nothing.

"He could hear the footsteps coming, but he never saw it on the camera," Kennedy said.

One other hot spot on Kennedy's haunted tour is the cafeteria, where unseen hands neatly stack the coins and bills in the safe each night.

Hastings College

A long-standing tradition in the theater involves keeping a ghost light lit in the building at all times.

Even after the building is closed for the night and all mortals have left, many theaters leave a light on as a gesture to any otherworldly inhabitants that they are welcome in the building. After all, the only time the lights are turned off is when the building is empty. It would be considered rude to turn off all the lights if someone or something was still in residence.

David Lower, a former theater and arena manager who now is production manager at the Fox Theatre in Detroit, notes "The ghost light is a tradition in the theater. A lot of the theaters that have a ghost light keep one on like a night light. The light is kept on for the comfort of the ghost and to acknowledge the building is occupied."

Taking that tradition one step further, the former music professor who haunts Hastings College's music building often appears there in the form of a ghost light. He also has appeared in human form, strolling the halls. Lights that turn themselves off and on also have been attributed to him.

New Hampshire

Keene State College

Harriet Huntress haunts the college, or at least many people believe she does. A few have attempted to refute her legend, but others are steadfast believers in the tales about her that have been told to freshmen for generations.

"I'm sure people want to believe in ghosts, or at least don't want them debunked. Don't we all like a mystery?" said Director of College Relations Michael Matros.

Harriet was a Concord resident and a power player in the state department of education in the twenties. Keene State Normal School named the hall after her for her statewide contributions to education.

Apparently, she became fond of the building, because in death, Harriet is said to race down the floors of the dormitory that bears her name. Sometimes she drags chains; other times she rides in a wheelchair. The wheelchair, as the legend goes, is kept in the attic in a steel cage. Harriet mainly confines her spectral activities to the top floor, but has been known to wander off on occasion.

Student journalists Steve Gordon and Stacy Milbour researched Harriet for the school paper in the seventies. They found the wheelchair belonged to someone else, but Harriet commandeered it when she was angry about the misbehavior of the dorm residents. Others hold that Miss Huntress first started making noise when women were kicked out of the dorm and the first male students were allowed to overnight in her dorm during World War II.

In the fall of 1970, Carle Hall, originally a men's dorm, became coed and Huntress again became a women's dorm. With that change, the ghost became more active.

Peter Lambert, a member of the Class of 2000, set out to refute the legend of Harriet Huntress' ghost, even though he disclosed he enjoyed spreading the tales to incoming freshmen.

"Students like ghost stories because what they're supposed to be doing with their college lives is thinking, analyzing, picking things apart, being logical," Matros said. "Ghost stories turn all that upside down and maybe that's refreshing. At Keene State, which isn't as old as New England colleges go, students take hold of older buildings and any thread of a haunting they find, hence the ghost of Ms. Huntress."

Students there also talk of the Phantom of Brickyard Pond.

On certain nights, when conditions are just right, one can see a phantom horse glowing through the water of the pond with a pair of young lovers trapped together forever in their watery grave.

Dartmouth College

Lucky 7's? Not for seven fraternity brothers who died of carbon monoxide poisoning at the Theta Chi fraternity. They – and two other men who were visiting the house – died in their sleep when a fissure developed in their coal furnace's flue pipe in February 1934.

It was little wonder that few cared to stay there after the incident, and the house, except for a section of the basement, was demolished in the fifties. Later, the Alpha Theta fraternity built a house on the site. Students say they get an eerie feeling in the old section of the basement. Additionally, the Theta Chi seven have shown up every once in a while at the frat house. People who have seen the apparitions picked their faces out of the 1934 issue of the *Aegis*, the college yearbook.

University of New Hampshire

The apparition of a despondent student who killed himself in the basement of Hetzel Hall occasionally stops by to visit the current residents. Students who live in the hall say they have awakened to see a young man standing over them, watching silently. Others have come home to the dorm to find their belongings moved and the room rearranged.

Similar happenings also have been witnessed in Congreve Hall, the scene of another hopeless student's suicide.

New Jersey

Drew University

Certainly not haunted, but pretty ghastly nonetheless is the university library's prize acquisition of 2002: a finger of well-respected British evangelist George Whitefield, who lived in the 1700s. School officials declined to speculate which digit they acquired and how they are certain the finger is Whitefield's.

Another odd acquisition at the university is Carol, who jumped from the fourth floor of Hoyt-Browne Hall to end her life, but now lives there forever. She's so well known, she's even touted on the college's website.

The dorm's other inhabitants are juniors and seniors. The fourth floor is a women-only hall, so Carol resides among the other women there. She also amuses herself by rearranging the furniture when the students are away.

New Mexico

New Mexico State University

Rhodes-Garrett-Hamiel, the oldest residence hall on campus, is home to many NMSU students, and a pair of ghosts.

Having a ghost in the residence hall improves its appeal to students, says Bob Smiggen, director of housing and dining services at the university. Even the hall's website proudly proclaims their ghostly resident.

The two-story, Spanish-style building was built by the Works Progress Administration. The Garrett wing, complete with a tower, is where the ghosts have taken up residence. Smiggen, who has been at NMSU for thirty-two years – half of that time in his current role – knows the students and the ghosts who live among them.

One of the ghosts thrives in the laundry room.

"People have put their laundry in," he says. "When they come back later, their laundry is done and folded in their baskets."

Smiggen says most people on campus believe one of two stories about how the ghosts came into residence there. In one, a young woman committed suicide in the building and her spirit never left. In the other version, a young woman died as the result of a fall down the stairway to the laundry room.

Though the stories have been widely accepted, Smiggen says, they are both fiction. There have been no deaths in the residence hall. Still, the ghostly activity continues.

"People say that lights are turned off and on in the building when there is no one there," he said.

Students like the stories so much, they sometimes go investigate. Everyone, Smiggen says, knows someone who has seen, felt, or heard the ghosts. Occasionally there are even ghost hunts.

"I think that at one time a student could go up into the tower, but with the pigeons and bat guano, the university closed it," he said. "No one is allowed up there because it is a health hazard."

Despite the ghostly goings-on, Rhodes-Garrett-Hamiel is a residence hall with a very active population. Smiggen credits that sense of community to the design of the building, which gives students an ample opportunity to study, socialize and tell stories.

"It is where people want to live, especially freshmen," he said. "The students kind of keep (the ghost stories) going. Some years, it's more than others; it just depends on who is there."

New York

New York University

On March 25, 1911, almost ten minutes before the bell signifying the end of the work day was scheduled to ring, the first cries of "Fire!" rang out on the eighth floor of the Asch Building in Greenwich Village. Because it was a Saturday, the only people in the ten-story building were workers at the Triangle Shirtwaist Company.

Triangle Shirtwaist was a common type of manufacturing company for the times, taking huge advantage of cheap immigrant labor.

"It was a sweatshop," novelist and screenwriter Rita Mae Brown says somberly.

The overwhelming majority of workers there were young women ages fifteen to twenty-three, who had immigrated from Europe – mostly Italy and Russia with many other countries thrown in – and had come to the United States with dreams for a better life. Instead they found themselves laboring from before sunrise to after sundown to support their families.

On that horrible Saturday afternoon, the young women heard the screams and bolted from their work stations at the cutting and sewing tables at the ten-year old building, but they found few ways to escape. The stairs were engulfed in flames. The front fire escape had been bolted shut by management to lessen theft and prevent weary workers from slipping outside for a breath of fresh air and a moment's rest. The back fire escape was unlocked but collapsed as the terrified women poured down the stairs, sending them crashing to their death on the sidewalk below. For most, the choice was clear – and horrifying. They could stay and burn to death or jump at least eight floors to the sidewalks below.

The fire spread with stunning speed, engulfing the eighth, ninth and tenth floors. There were no fire extinguishers, ceiling sprinklers or alarms – none were required by the laws of the day. Fire trucks responded, but their ladders didn't reach any further than the sixth floor. Bystanders watched in horror as workers jumped to their deaths, some of them falling upon on-lookers who were attempting to provide aid.

The fire was brief but intense. The blaze exhausted itself in thirty minutes. By nightfall, the sidewalks were soaked from the fire hoses and littered with piles of charred bodies. The heavy stench of burned flesh hung in the air. Exhausted students from New York University's law school tried to regain their strength as they surveyed the carnage. They helped fire fighters rescue 130 workers from the building, but 146 perished in the blaze.

"Many people were trapped inside," Brown says. "Some jumped to their deaths. Others were trapped inside and burned to death."

The tragedy became a national catalyst for workplace reform. As a result, a shorter work week was enacted, as were sweeping fire and safety regulations. But not everyone was satisfied with the reforms in the aftermath of the tragedy.

The building was sold to New York University, renamed the Brown Building, and now houses classrooms, laboratories, offices, and includes the university's central supply office. To this day, some workers and students avoid the building, particularly at night. They say the spirits of the victims are still restless and dissatisfied, even after seventy years. The paranormal activity practically makes the air crackle with electricity.

"That part of NYU is emphatically haunted," says Brown, who completed the final two years' work on her bachelor's degree there. "I believe it's haunted. You could feel it. I took French classes there and could never learn a darn thing. I couldn't concentrate. No wonder I could never get my pronunciation right."

One day in 2000, smoke detectors at the university's Main Building went off unexpectedly, probably triggered by dust particles stirred up by construction workers. Curiously, a few moments later, the alarms in the Brown went off as well. Were the spirits trying to be heard?

Elsewhere on campus, residents in the 930-student Third North Dormitory, an undergraduate facility built in 1988 have reported a variety of phenomena, from items suddenly sliding across the room to doors slamming shut or shaking violently. No incidents have occurred at the building to provide historical context to explain the happenings.

Marymount College

One night, during the late sixties, a group of students gathered in Sacre Coeur dormitory, lovingly called "Sacky." They had gathered to compile a story of the dorm's ghostly history, particularly a tale about the children of the last family to own the building before it came into the college's possession. The oldest son threw himself under the wheels of a train and his sister, distraught at her brother's violent, surprising death, went permanently insane. Later, the family's youngest son hanged himself in Sacky's attic.

Legend has it that the youngest son's ghost appears each night on the anniversary of his death, as he is reputed to have done that night. Since that night in the sixties, students have commemorated the date, which comes near the end of the school year, with a full house party, complete with skeletons, Ouija boards, and other ghostly trappings.

Niagara University

Located on a ridge high above the Niagara gorge and world-famous Niagara Falls, Niagara University is just a mile from the Canadian border and hardly seems the place for ghosts, but one dogged spirit is said to persist there. From 1856 to 1931, the college was known as Seminary of Angels.

One of the seminarians in the school's early days perished in an 1864 fire at Clet Hall dormitory as he attempted to check the rooms and make sure everyone had been evacuated. Some say he's still on duty, appearing to wayward students, making them change their ways. Occasionally, he also pulls a prank or two, just to keep things light.

Nyack College

The medieval-designed Shuman Building is the college's administration building, but the circular room at the top is not the place to be at night. There, playful and pesky spirits fiddle with the lights. Custodial workers say they turn off all the lights when they leave at night, but staff and administrators say the lights are ablaze when they arrive early in the morning.

Rensselaer Polytechnic Institute

West Hall originally had functioned as a hospital during the Civil War. Down in the bowels of the hospital was the ward for soldiers who had suffered from mental and emotional disorders as a result of their war experiences. Local legend persists that West Hall is home to "Betsy," the ghost of a nurse who had tended to the insane patients and had gone insane herself. If you listen closely, they say, you can hear her muttering to herself as she makes her rounds.

Skidmore College

In 1970, a fire broke out on the first floor of the Wilmarth Hall dormitory, which had been completed only two years earlier. The physical damage was relatively minor, but the human cost was grave. One student at the then all-female college had been killed in the blaze, the result of being thrown against a wall by a vicious back draft. Residents of the dorm say they sometimes see her walking about the dorm, making mysterious tapping noises.

Moore Hall, named for Henry T. Moore, who served thirty-two years as the college's second president, is built on hallowed Indian burial grounds. The spirits there are said to be so powerful and upset, they swallowed up a bulldozer and its operator who were clearing the grounds for the dormitory site.

Union College

An entryway to Jackson's Gardens, the formal gardens near the center of campus in New York's first regents' college, established 1795, beckons visitors to "Climb high, climb far, your goal the sky, your aim the star." When daylight turns to night, however, the gardens are watched over by the ghost of a deaf professor who was bedeviled by his boisterous students.

The campus' most famous ghost is Alice van der Veer, who met her fate at the end of a rope or in flames in Jackson Gardens.

The lovely daughter of Jan van der Veer, a rawboned Dutch colonist who spurned all the suitors who attempted the woo her, Alice double-crossed her father after he surprised her and her boyfriend as they smooched on the banks of the Mohawk River in July 1672. Townspeople heard the shots and came running. They found the corpse of the young man, Alice, and her angry, overbearing father dragging her away. The mob turned unruly, thinking the father to be evil. They captured him and immediately burned him at the stake. Alice, now without a father and a lover, became hysterical and the mob decided she was evil, too. They pursued her and caught her at the site where Jackson's Gardens are now. She met her fate by hanging or at the stake.

Alice is said to return to the campus on the first full moon of each July. She's recognizable by the bruise on her neck and her moans and wails as she walks along the banks of the Mohawk River, looking for her departed lover.

United States Military Academy

Discipline, of course, is an important part of life for the cadets at West Point. It appears to be for the spirits who are said to live there, too.

In the early 1970s, several cadets in dorm room 4714 of the 47th Division barracks were treated to a display of ghostly hijinks in their room. Items moved around in their room, the water in their bathroom shower changed from hot to cold and back again without reason. And finally, the cadets say, after the temperature in the room took a quick dip, a specter clad in Civil War soldier's garb made a brief appearance. The cadets informed their superiors, who initially dismissed their experiences as a prank, but agreed to spend a night in the room to see for themselves. The apparition made itself apparent to them as well. A midshipman from the rival U.S. Naval Academy later admitted to playing a prank on the cadets, but West

Point of officials rebuffed his claim, saying his explanation was not plausible.

Another apparition is said to have inhabited the superintendent's home, where the housekeeping staff was upset over unseen visitors who crept into the splendid home's downstairs bedroom to muss the bed linens the housekeeping staff had taken such pains to keep neat.

Wells College

It's amazing that the spirits don't trip over each other as they elbow each other around the campus.

Wells was founded in 1868 by Henry Wells, founder of Wells Fargo and American Express. Several times in the college's early years, influenza epidemics struck the campus, taking a terrible toll on the women. Two of the college's ghost stories come from those epidemics.

During one, afflicted women were brought to a hospital ward set up on the fourth floor of the college's Main Building, now a dormitory. There they were ministered to by a corps of nurses, but there was little the nurses could do but make them comfortable until the inevitable came. Because it was winter, transporting the bodies out was prohibitive, so a room was set aside as a temporary morgue. The door to the room was painted red.

After the epidemic, the hospital ward and the morgue were no longer needed, so the beds were removed and the red door was painted over. Some time later, students were shocked to see the red paint bleeding through, and many took it as a symbol of the tragedy that had happened there. No records exist about which room was used as the morgue, but students still surreptitiously check the doors on that floor for signs of red paint.

During another epidemic, Main Building was again transformed into a makeshift hospital, but this time, the third and fourth floors were pressed into service and again many nurses were called in to help. A fire broke out in the hall and the nurses worked hard to pull out as many of the women they could. In the process, many of the nurses were overcome by the smoke and flames, and perished.

Today, students living on those floors report they sometimes wake up feeling as though they'd just had their heads stroked, faces wiped or had otherwise been ministered to by a nurse.

Built in 1890, Main Building is now Main Hall, the largest residence hall on campus.

The bonds forged in dorms sometimes last throughout lifetimes, but the ties between three seniors in Pettibone House, lasted even longer.

Pettibone House was originally the home of the George S. Pettibone family, constructed in 1857. Its size made it particularly appropriate as a residence hall for upperclassmen, and particularly homelike.

The three seniors were returning to school from spring break. As the first two to arrive unpacked, the third entered, looking particularly troubled. Her roommates asked her what was the matter and she poured out her fears that after graduation, they'd go their own ways and lose touch with each other. The two comforted her and assured her they would always stay in touch.

Relieved, she wandered from the room to attend to other matters. After some time passed, the two remaining roommates were summoned to the dean of students' office. There, the grim-faced dean gently informed them their roommate was dead, killed in a traffic accident on her way to the campus from spring break.

The car had her luggage and personal effects in it. She had not arrived at the campus.

Among the crowd of permanent residents on campus are:

• The ghost of a security guard who died as he tried to evacuate a burning dorm and still keeps watch over Morgan Hall, the building constructed at the site of the tragedy.

• The ghost of a student who dabbled in the occult as a way to help lift her out of depression. She is rarely seen, but cold spots in Room 220 of Main Hall prove her presence. The room now houses an RA.

North Carolina

Chowan College

The Brown Lady makes her home at Chowan College's McDowell Columns Hall

Eolene Davidson looked almost as though she had been cast of Dresden china. Tall and slender, she was a blue-eyed brunette with beautiful fair skin, a winning personality and a knack for making friends. She seemed to naturally gravitate toward people, and they seemed to fall easily under her charm and warmth.

Eolene had the world before her. The only child of a wealthy North Carolina farmer, she was committed to fulfilling a promise to her parents before she married a prominent New York attorney, James Lorrene. The promise was to complete her education at Chowan Female Institute.

In a summer during the late 1870s or early 1880s, she arrived in Murfreesboro for the start of classes. After her bout of homesickness passed, she found college suited her well, both in the classroom and among her classmates. They soon noticed Eolene was at her most radiant when she wore a beautiful, sheer brown ensemble. The fabric made a delicate but distinctive rustle as she walked, heralding her arrival. Her friends dubbed her "the Lady in Brown."

Eolene returned for her sophomore year with renewed enthusiasm and purpose, but fell ill in mid-October. Despite the fervent prayers of her friends and the ministrations of doctors and nurses, her fever grew worse. On October 31, she succumbed. Her body was sent home to Northampton County the next day.

Ask almost anyone on campus today where to look for the Lady in Brown and you'll get the same answer: "The fourth floor of the Columns Building," a campus security officer directed. "I had heard stories about her even before I started working here. I've heard lots more since then."

In earlier years, many reported a glimpse of the Lady in Brown including founding principal Dr. Archibald McDowell and a science professor named Dr. Delk. In later years, she has remained out of sight, but the familiar rustle of her favorite brown ensemble is often heard. She has made herself present in other ways, by knocking on doors and turning lights on and off.

In years past, upperclassmen would roust freshmen at midnight on or near October 31 to search for the Lady in Brown in the dorm. In 1925, students voted to make one final search for her, and toured the campus with her. After their rounds of the campus were complete, they made a bonfire at a nearby ravine and committed the Lady in Brown to it. After the embers from the bonfire had cooled, they were placed in a bottle, sealed and stored away.

But the Lady in Brown was not so easily dispatched. The Columns building became a men's dorm when the college went coed in the late fifties. Their rite of exorcism was to make the old girl walk the plank in effigy for 1958's homecoming festivities.

Today the building is officially the McDowell-Columns Building, home to the college's administrative offices and bookstore. The fourth floor is still a residential floor – for faculty, staff, and one very loyal spirit.

Davidson College

As one of the nation's foremost liberal arts colleges, one would expect Davidson to have a ghost that's a cut above the rest...and it is. It's a ghost building.

Chambers Hall, the college's original classroom building, burned down in 1921. The second Chambers was built over the spot where the first one had stood.

"In dry seasons, the footprint and columns of the original building can be seen – it's almost as though the imprint burns its way from the ground up into the grass," said Jan Blodgett, the college's archivist and records management coordinator.

Visitors to the college can climb to Chambers' second floor and look out toward the front campus to catch a glimpse.

Ohio

Ohio State University

A woman in pink eternally gains revenge by haunting Pomerene Hall.

"The story goes that a faculty member of the university became more and more despondent, working longer and longer hours," said Dorrie Wells, operations administrator for the School of Physical Activity and Educational Services. "He became suicidal and committed suicide on the knoll behind Pomerene Hall. His wife, the Pink Lady, claimed she would not let the university forget what they did to her husband and has been haunting the Mirror Lake hollow ever since."

Dressed perpetually in a pink party dress, the woman glides across room 213 in Pomerene Hall to a window, and then vanishes.

Room 213 was once the site of afternoon teas and elaborate events. Young women and men danced and frolicked there, watched by chaperones who had their own hidden entry door. The room is now a dance studio and the chaperones' entry door – now equipped with a handle and lock – make the door no longer a secret. It still provides excellent access to the room for the living – and others.

The window of Room 213 overlooks Mirror Lake, home to a much more visible ghost. She dresses in costumes fashionable in the 30s, including a warming muff for her hands. She is the ghost most often reported on campus, though few have heard of her. Is it a coincidence she haunts the very location that can be seen from the home of the university's other well-known apparition?

"People claim they have seen the form of a woman in a long pink gown floating across the water," Wells said. "This apparition is seen mostly during the late fall and winter to early spring. Most claims are by students strolling through Mirror Lake in the late evening and at night when there is a moon. She appears as a light pink-tinted mist that eventually resembles the form of a woman in a long, flowing dress, not real distinct, but identifiable."

Wells said she is not usually on campus when the Lady of the Lake appears and when she first heard the story, did not believe it. Events that occurred one evening in the late 1980s have caused her to change her mind.

"I was just enjoying the late evening and walking my dog before I went home," she said. "The dog became very interested in the knoll area. So naturally, I was wondering what he saw. A pink mist appeared and floated down to Mirror Lake."

Wells, who works in Pomerene Hall, said many of her co-workers report hearing strange footsteps at night.

"One can hear the steps going up a staircase," she said. "They run to follow and not find anyone else in the hall or adjacent rooms. Students and faculty alike have claimed to try to follow the steps that just go up one staircase and down another and no matter how fast one tries to intercept, they can never catch up to the sound or find anyone. I have personally heard this as well as locking up rooms only to find them standing open shortly after. Still locked, but standing open."

Wells says the Pink Lady has entered the technological age.

"Another department in the college had a computer talking to them," she said. "Several people came in late one Saturday evening and had their computers say 'Hello, hello.' This totally unnerved them. We all figured it was the Pink Lady."

Baldwin-Wallace College

In its first life in the 1850s, Kohler Hall served as the first Methodist Children's Home. Later enlarged from two to three stories, the building was acquired by the college for use as a dormitory. In 1940, it was named for Josephine Kohler, who provided funds for a complete renovation of the building.

A mysterious blue haze is said to have appeared several times in the hall. During its appearances, the haze apparently liked to get up close and personal with the students whose rooms it visited, occasionally leaving them gasping for breath in its wake.

Bowling Green State University

A ghost named Alice haunts the Joe E. Brown and Eva Marie Saint theaters in University Hall, built in 1915, the oldest building on campus.

Alice is said to have been a coed who died as the result of an accident during her performance in "Othello." Stage managers make a point of verbally inviting her to all performances, saving her a seat and always leaving a light burning on stage for her. If the ritual is neglected in any way, the theater makes itself vulnerable to her loud noises, set problems, and electrical woes.

Another ghost haunts the Chi Omega sorority house on the west side of the campus. The apparition's name is Amanda and she is believed to be a freshman who died in a train accident on the night she was to pledge the sorority.

Kenyon College

Even in the grainy, indistinct photographs of the day, it was clear that Stuart Lathrop Pierson was a handsome young man. Yet Pierson gained an unfortunate distinction at what should have been one of the crowning moments of his young life.

In October 1905, he became the first fatality resulting from fraternity hazing. Pierson's mangled body was discovered alongside train tracks at the edge of a bridge crossing the Kokosing River. Whether he was tied to the tracks, tied and placed on the tracks, or simply hit as he sat on the tracks as he had supposedly been instructed by the Delta Kappa Epsilon brothers, remains a matter of debate to this day.

Three days before Halloween, the anniversary of his death, Pierson makes an appearance from the fourth floor of Old Kenyon dormitory.

Another site of interest is the Shaffer Pool, home to some odd phenomena. Unseen hands turn the pool lights and sound system on and off, and a disembodied voice has been heard counting off laps to swimmers. Wet footprints have been discovered when staff members open the pool in the morning. Few people want to see anything change, however. Whatever causes these things to happen seems to have an affinity for the home team and a distaste for visiting swim teams.

Marietta College

George is the nickname of the resident spirit at the Alpha Xi Delta sorority house. Just who George is, though, is the matter of some debate. He could have been the house's original owner, a guest who died there, or a peripatetic spirit who wandered in from the historic cemetery next door.

Founded in 1797 and chartered in 1835, Marietta had many students, faculty members, and staff walk through its halls. It's understandable if a few want to linger a while longer.

Miami University

One of the handful of colleges that offer their campus ghostlore on the Internet, MU's site (www.lib.muohio.edu/mysteries/), complete with archival photographs, newspaper clippings, correspondence, and succinct vignettes, is a winner.

One of the popular tales is of the Oxford ghost rider, a Miami University student who was riding a motorcycle to his girlfriend's home to propose marriage. He is said to have missed a turn near her home and was thrown into a barbed wire fence, which decapitated him. Students still travel to the site to complete his ride, and in doing so, they say, they can see the headlight and taillight of his motorcycle.

Sinclair Community College

The college's Blair Hall Theatre was constructed on land used many years earlier as an execution ground and people say they have heard the sounds of muffled conversations, sobbing, and doors slamming.

Wittenberg University

If the legend is true, a group of Wittenberg students went a step better than the film "Animal House."

As a prank, they led a horse up the steps of Myers Hall, the school's oldest building, to the cupola. When they'd finished their tomfoolery, they all headed downstairs – all except the horse, that is. They tried everything they could think of to coax the animal down the stairway, but the animal wouldn't budge. As the minutes turned to hours, the pranksters grew more fearful about the repercussions that could await them and resorted to drastic action – shooting the animal.

Built in 1846 and originally used as a multi-purpose building, Myers Hall is now a coed dorm, home to the university's sesquicentennial bell and an equine ghost. Students say they can still hear the doomed steed's hooves in the stairwell at night.

Oklahoma

Oklahoma State University

Ghost towns – windswept relics of the golden days of cowboy culture – are common in Oklahoma. At Oklahoma State University's campus in Stillwater, ghosts are almost as plentiful.

Students living in Cordell Hall have named the specter that haunts their hall Cordello. Opened in 1939, Cordell is known for sounds in the ceiling where no pipes or ducts exist.

Light fixtures have been known to go off and on by themselves. Students have reported feeling as if someone was following them through the halls and even felt a tap on the shoulder, but when they turned to see who it was, they were alone.

Clearly Cordello is a friendly spirit who just likes to make his presence known.

Other permanent residents of the campus include:

• Fred, who lives in the Edmon Low Library. Custodians working the night shift have reported being touched on the shoulder or hearing a disembodied voice softly murmur their names.

• Architect Joseph Foucart, designer of Old Williams Hall, one of the first buildings constructed on campus, where the Seretean Center now stands. An eccentric in life, Foucart was buried in an inaccessible Williams courtyard. It was a maze of narrow corridors, dead-end hallways and odd-shaped rooms.

Oregon

Pacific University

Vera, a playful ghost with the tiniest of crushes on a Pacific University staff member, haunts Knight Hall.

The ghost's singing and piano playing can be heard echoing through the building's halls. In the sixties, security officers investigating the melodies encountered the form of a woman enveloped in shimmering blue light. In the eighties, the spirit apparently grew stronger, and even voiced its displeasure at some students' keyboard performances. Students, faculty, staff, and members of the media have witnessed Vera's presence.

Jeff Grundon, the university's assistant director of athletics and admissions, has experienced the phenomena several times and is convinced there is a ghost at Knight Hall.

"The first one appeared July 5 several years ago when the admissions office had just moved into Knight Hall," Grundon said. "I had come back one evening with a torchiere lamp. I was putting it together in my new office. It was about 7:30 on a pretty warm night. I had the window open in the office and a hot breeze was blowing in. I felt somebody staring at me and the hair on the back of my neck was standing up. I turned around and there was no one there."

Another evening, Grundon was again working late. He was walking down the hall to the room where the office mail was kept. The fire door had been propped open with a wooden doorstop.

"The door had a bell on it and the door started to move across the floor with the wooden doorstop on it, but the bell didn't ring," he said. "Anytime anyone grabbed that door, the bell would tinkle. As soon as I looked at it and tried to pull it open, it was as if someone was holding onto the other side. I finally freed it and thought 'I'm going to get out of here.'"

Before his first few encounters with Vera, Grundon said he did not believe in ghosts, even though he grew up in Hawaii, where otherworldly spirits are an accepted part of the culture.

"I was a total non-believer," he said. His views changed after working in Knight Hall for a while.

The next encounter was more pronounced. Grundon's supervisor left the restroom, which was right outside Grundon's office. Grundon, who had been chatting with a colleague in the adjacent hallway, turned to enter the restroom and found it locked.

"I asked my boss if she had locked the door and she said she hadn't," Grundon said. "I kept working with it and I had the handle all the way down and suddenly it flew open."

Vera seems to have an attachment to Grundon. She sometimes turns his space heater on and off, or flips on the fan. She'd sometimes pace the hallway outside his office or walk up and down the stairwell next to his office.

"I would yell, 'Hey Vera, knock it off. I don't have time to play today,'" he said. It seemed to do the trick.

Grundon got ribbed by his colleagues because Vera was such a good buddy....or maybe more.

He'd leave his office long after his colleagues had left and stop off at a nearby store before going home. On the way out of the building, he'd methodically work his way through the building, turning off the lights. But moments later, while driving past the building on the way out of the parking lot, he'd see every light in the building turned on.

"At the time, I think I was the only male in the building," he said. "It was me and seventeen women. I was the only single guy."

Vera also would cause unexplained foul smells next to Grundon's desk. The smells were so strong, they were still evident if the windows were open and the fans were turned on. Grundon said he knew it was her because he could always sense her presence.

"Whenever she was around, the hair on the back of my neck would stand up," he said.

"One day I was in my office reading a file and happened to glance down at my briefcase and it moved about three feet all by itself," he said. "I ran next door and told my boss she was never going to believe what had just happened."

Luckily for Grundon, most of the folks in Knight Hall do believe in Vera. One of Grundon's colleagues used to ride his bike to and from work, keeping it stored in the basement of the building during the day. One evening he got all the way downstairs when he realized he had forgotten his backpack.

"He said something like 'oh shit,' and went up the stairwell. He heard footsteps coming up behind him and he turned to look, but he saw nothing," Grundon recalled. "He had the door open a little bit, but when he tried to push the door open further, he couldn't. Finally, it flew open. He went upstairs, got his backpack and was out of there."

Another staff member was in a room with several shelves mounted on a wall. On those shelves were plastic bins. All at once, the bins flew off the shelves and the shelves came off the wall.

"It wasn't like they fell," Grundon said. "They flew off."

One of the current assistant basketball coaches, then a work-study student for Grundon, used to try to contact Vera with a Ouija board. He and some of the other basketball players would borrow Grundon's keys and squeeze into a little room that has since been taken off-line. There they would have discussions with her through the Ouija board. They learned she was killed when she was eighteen and there were two other spirits in the house with them. Since Vera is a very good, strong spirit, she is able to keep the other two in check and won't allow other spirits in the building.

"She wants attention. She wants people to care about her," Grundon said.

Pennsylvania

Bucks County Community College

Historic Tyler Hall at Bucks County Community College was built of pink sandstone quarried from the estate

When Stella Elkins and George Frederick Tyler wed, it was as much a merger as a marriage. The Elkins family was prominent in the railroad industry. Tyler, a financier, came from a family active in the petroleum industry.

The Tyler-Elkins union bonded into a family, as Stella and George eventually became parents to three children and enjoyed a prosperous, philanthropic but unpretentious life largely outside the eyes of the public.

George Tyler, who served as the state commander of the American Legion, suffered a kidney injury during World War I and was slowed somewhat by it throughout the remainder of his life, though he managed to remain active in a variety of outdoor pursuits.

Stella Tyler was an active, energetic woman. She served as a member of Temple University's board of trustees and was an excellent artist and sculptor. Her artistic talents were honed and her sculpture inspired by Boris Blai, a protégé of Auguste Rodin.

In 1927, the Tylers began work on a country home north of Philadelphia. Work was completed in 1930, but the sixty-room French-Norman mansion was largely secluded in the heavy woods, hidden from the local citizens. The home had been constructed of pink sandstone quarried from the estate. Two hundred masons were brought over from Italy to do the job right. The oak paneling in the grand home was purchased from a home in New England and painstakingly installed. The grand house was the first mansion in North America to be air-conditioned, but precious few locals were invited in to feel the cool air.

"It was closed off from the rest of the world," said Bucks County Community College professor Douglas Rosentrater. "Either you worked here or you were invited here."

The grand home hugged the ground over an Indian council rock perched high on a sheer cliff above the Neshaminy River, sacred ground and treacherous terrain at the same time. Stairs lead down from the cliff and beckon visitors to wander, to come look for arrowheads and small carvings.

"It starts out very pleasant at first," Rosentrater says. "But very quickly, you have to make a decision about whether you want to continue on."

Several who elected to do so met their deaths as a result, he says.

George Tyler quietly bought up local farms to increase his land holdings to 2,000 acres. He hired the former owners to work the land as tenant farmers. Tyler was a generous and thoughtful employer, making sure each of the tenant farmers' homes was converted to electrical power and equipped with indoor plumbing. Tyler started a dairy and ran a pair of mills. The community around the estate was prosperous, content, and unbeknownst to many, wealthy and powerful friends such as President Franklin Roosevelt, sometimes stopped in for dinner. Roosevelt visited the mansion at least three times.

A tall, lithe woman with brown hair and penetrating blue eyes, Stella Tyler was a versatile and talented artist. She created beautiful, intricate tapestries for the home, including one in the entryway. In 1951 she began sculpting under Blai's tutelage, and became wildly prolific working in bronze. She also was a talented musician.

"She was an insomniac," says Eileen Zolotorofe, special projects coordinator for the Bucks County Community College Foundation. "She had a baby grand piano and she'd slip down to the music room and play when she couldn't sleep."

George died in 1947 and Stella lived on to 1963. During their lives, they had given one of the homes, Georgian Terrace, to Temple University. Upon their death, they gave the Newtown house to the university as well.

The Tyler home didn't fit into Temple's plans, but Bucks County rather quickly saw potential for a community college. Pennsylvania's community college system was in its infancy and Bucks County was ahead of the wave. An agreement giving Temple $700,000 for 200 acres and the buildings was finalized on June 21, 1965. Another $300,000 in renovations fitted the mansion for its new purpose. For $1 million, Bucks County became home to one of the loveliest community colleges in the nation.

When construction began on Penn Hall, a modern classroom building, whispers began to circulate that many of Stella's lesser sculptures had been dumped into the forms where the cement for the foundation was poured. The rumor was confirmed by the contractors and some wonder if that is the reason Stella, an insomniac during her lifetime, still walks the hall at night, looking for her sculptures. Custodial staff and others have reported feeling a presence in Tyler Hall, particularly on the third floor, and also the walkway to the Orangery. Others say she ruffles the curtains and rattles the windows. A few have reported feeling a cold, lifeless hand on their shoulder, only to turn in horror and see nothing.

"I have had strange, interesting things happen to me in Tyler," says Sandra Sobek-Allen, a longtime college security officer.

Once, early in her employment, Sobek-Allen was entering the pub area of the building and encountered a delightful scent.

"It was the tremendously fragrant smell of a big dinner," she said. "It was like a turkey dinner you'd make for Thanksgiving, with baked apples."

Sobek-Allen said she knew immediately she was not alone.

"I said 'holy sugar…hi, Stella!'

"You could feel the presence," she said. "I was not afraid; I was peaceful. She was welcoming me to her home. That's the way she was doing it."

Bloomsburg University

Ned, the gloomy ghost of the Haas Center for the Arts, usually just sits quietly, but has a presence about him that lets others know he's there. Sometimes, though, when he's feeling extra low, he's been known to bleat in despair, an eerie sound that had unnerved actors and technicians.

Ned is believed to have been part of a dance troupe that performed at the university in the 1970s.

Cedar Crest College

Butz Hall sits at the middle of Cedar Crest College's neat-as-a-bandbox campus in Allentown

Has anyone seen Wanda? She's reputed to be the ghost of Butz Hall on this friendly, neat-as-a-bandbox Allentown campus. There seems to be no factual basis for her, and no record of her death, just the enduring scuttlebutt of late-night talk in the dorms. Still the legend of unhappy Wanda seems as firmly rooted there as the evergreens on the commons, and let's face it, every college needs at least one ghost to call its own.

Dickinson College

The Robert A. Waidner Admissions House was once the home of a prosperous banker, but when times turned hard, he couldn't accept his fall from prominence and loss of face in the community. He decided suicide was his only alternative. As his wife, children and friends enjoyed a party on the house's ground floor, he shot himself in his third-floor office. His footsteps are still heard on that floor today.

Gettysburg College and Lutheran Theological Seminary

Old Main Hall, just off Gettysburg's Seminary Ridge, is now the Simon Schmucker Hall at Lutheran Theological Seminary.

No matter where one travels in Gettysburg, from the center of town at rush hour to battlefield sites such as the Devil's Den and Little Round Top, the atmosphere seems eternally muted, a reflection by many, no doubt, of the gravity of the events that transformed a town of 2,400 to the site of the War Between the States' most decisive battlefields.

Gettysburg College and the Lutheran Theological Seminary once made up Pennsylvania College. Formerly known as the Old Dorm, Pennsylvania Hall now serves as the administrative headquarters of Gettysburg College.

The Old Dorm at Pennsylvania College served as a hospital during the Civil War. It is now the administrative building for Gettysburg College.

Below:
Stevens Hall, which served as a prep school for Gettysburg College, is home to a vain ghost who primps in a mirror.

At the seminary, the building now known as Samuel Simon Schmucker Hall was Old Main, the oldest building in America dedicated to Lutheran theological education. During the three days of battle in Gettysburg – July 1 through 3, 1863 – and for weeks afterward, both buildings were pressed into service as hospitals. Schmucker Hall also served as a lookout station.

In the wake of the battle is a community of spirits unlike any other in America.

Here are some of the places they congregate:

• Surgery in those days was more art than science and the mortality rate was very high. Antiseptics, sulfa drugs, antibiotics and sterile technique had not yet been discovered. Surgical tools were crude. Direct hits to the head or torso almost always resulted in death. Injuries to the extremities usually resulted in the need for amputation. The overworked surgeons in the Old Dorm and Old Main worked long hours and moved quickly from patient to patient. The number of corpses and amputated limbs grew rapidly and their disposal became worrisome, particularly in the summer heat. A number of apparitions have been seen at these buildings, many in uniform.

• Stevens Hall was built after the battle and was used as a women's dorm and later as Gettysburg College's preparatory school. It is home to the apparition of a vain young woman who primps in the mirrors on the third floor.

Kutztown University

Mary is the resident apparition at Kutztown University's Old Main building.

Everyone seems to know of Mary, the apparition who makes her quarters on the fifth floor of the Old Main Building. But few people seem to know much about her, though. The speculation is ample: She was jilted, pregnant, depressed, terminally ill. She died of natural causes, suicide by hanging, or suicide by jumping down an elevator shaft. Over the years there have been reports of cold spots and the like, but little with any rhyme or reason. Was there really a Mary? Quite possibly, but what happened to her remains a mystery and maybe that's what keeps the story alive.

Moravian College

Main Hall, Brethren's House and Comenius Hall on the storybook college's South Campus all are said to be haunted, as is the Phi Mu Epsilon house, where the ghost of a young woman who was the victim of domestic violence remains.

Muhlenberg College

Sometimes, matching up a building and its ghostly occupant seems so easy. Take the ghost of Oscar Bernheim, the college's former registrar. He was said to have donated his home to the college after his death there, and apparently came by to check on things every now and again.

But things are not always what they seem, and not only in the spirit realm. Oscar Bernheim did indeed work for the college. During his tenure there, from 1907 to 1946, he served in many positions, including registrar. But upon investigation, college personnel say Bernhein probably did not live in the home.

"We are quite certain that he did not die there," said Christine Murphy, Muhlenberg's director of college communications.

But nowadays, the talk about Bernheim's ghost is probably moot. Bernheim House was razed in 1998 to make way for the Trexler Pavillion for Theatre and Dance, and whomever it is who was lurking around at Bernheim House seems to have vacated the neighborhood as well.

Penn State University

With the ink drying on his medical discharge from the Union Army in 1864, Colonel George Wiestling moved to Mont Alto, in south central Pennsylvania. He was a shareholder in the Mont Alto Iron Co. and moved there to become its last ironmaster.

Times were tough and the iron industry was in transition, so Wiestling bought a log cabin that had been built in 1807 and added on to it, to provide a home for his sisters and brother to live with him.

After his death, his estate was purchased by the state and his home became home to the Pennsylvania State Forest Academy.

"When the Pennsylvania Forestry School was here, the third floor was lined with bunks," says Dr. David Gnage, the campus' chief executive officer.

Since the merger of the forestry school with Pennsylvania State College in 1929, Wiestling Hall, the oldest building in the state's education system and the primary building on the Mont Alto campus, has seen a variety of uses – as a dining hall, dormitory, classroom building and its current use as administrative offices.

"As I understand it, the colonel's ghost is here as well as that of a young woman who was killed by her boyfriend some time after World War II," Gnage says.

A photo taken early in the 1900s showed a shadowy apparition, which many believe to be Wiestling, watching over the property. In the years since then, the colonel has stayed out of sight, but has been heard walking around the third floor at night and on the stairs heading toward the third floor. Noises in the kitchen and dining room also have been reported, and kitchen appliances have turned themselves on and off. The front door, even when barred, made unmistakable banging noises.

Wiestling Hall is one of many haunted Penn State sites. The Watts Hall dormitory at the university's University Park campus is haunted by the ghost of Old Coaly, a mule used to haul masonry supplies for the dorm's construction in the mid-91800s. When the mule died, his remains were stored in the Old Main building, but his braying is still reported.

Another University Park dormitory, Runkle Hall, has been the site of a bucking bed, loud noises and a voice that comes from seemingly nowhere.

Other ghostly sites include:

• The Beam Business Administration Building, a converted dormitory, has been the site of mild poltergeist activity.

• A pair of ghosts has been reported hovering in Schwab Theatre.

• The Old Botany Building is home of two spirits who have resided there since the mid-1800s.

• Students at Patee Library's second floor stacks, where a coed was stabbed to death in 1969, say unseen forces there give them the creeps and seem to suck the air out of the area, leaving them gasping for breath.

U.S. Army War College

With a history extending back to the mid-1700s, it's no wonder the campus now occupied by the U.S. Army War College at Carlisle Barracks is crawling with ghosts.

"Most of Carlisle is haunted, mostly on the south side of the post," said Allen Campbell, author of *Ghosts at Carlisle Barracks Army War College.*

"Why? Because most of the old buildings are still standing in the area, including the gym, the hospital, the Hessian powder magazine museum and housing and the printing press building that is now the Letort View Community Center, formerly the officers' club."

The facility has operated as the U.S. Army War College, the Army's senior educational facility, since 1951. Before that, it served a variety of functions, including: Adjutant General's School, Armed Forces Information School, Army Security Agency School (1949-1951), Carlisle Indian Industrial School (1879-1918), Center for Strategic Studies, Chaplain School, Combat Developments Command Institute of Advanced Studies, Medical Field Service School (1920-1946), Military Police School, School of Cavalry Practice and Strategic Studies Institute.

From Campbell's arrival there in 1992, things didn't seem quite right, he said

"I felt the place was strange, but didn't know why," he said. "Later I found out it was very haunted."

Among the haunted sites are:

• Ashburn Hall, built in 1908, formerly was used as a hospital and morgue, but now provides accommodations for visiting dignitaries. It has cold spots, lights that go on and off by themselves, and apparitions have been spotted there from time to time.

• At Letort View Community Center, lights, appliances and other electronic equipment turn on and off seemingly at will and phantom footsteps have been heard around the building.

• Coren Apartments previously served as a dormitory for students at the Carlisle Indian Industrial School. A young Sioux girl, Lucy Pretty Eagle, was among the students housed there. She died while at the school, was buried in the graveyard on campus and now haunts the building.

• The Carlisle Indian School's most illustrious graduate was undoubtedly Jim Thorpe, who attended school there from 1904 to 1909 and 1911 to 1913 before going on to win gold as decathlon and pentathlon champion at the 1912 Stockholm Olympics. The building that now houses Jim Thorpe Hall was originally built by Carlisle Indian students in 1887. Thorpe, who visited the gymnasium building often while a student, felt quite at home there, but Jim Thorpe Hall isn't the warm, inviting place to others as it was to track and field's greatest ironman. People working out report feeling uneasy there, as if they were under surveillance. Others have reported seeing a child-sized figure looking out from a second-story window.

University of Pittsburgh

Litchfield Tower B is a modern residence hall, but the residents wonder if there might be a ghost story in the making there. When women residents venture into the communal showers, they hear the disembodied sounds of sobbing and screaming.

Bruce Hall, converted from a hotel to a residence hall, is the center of most of the university's spirit activity with ghostly footsteps, eerie noises, furniture that rearranges itself and mild poltergeist activity

Widener University

Its reputation as a haunted building makes The Castle a popular place to live. Now home to a sorority, the building has documented cold spots throughout the building.

Rhode Island

Salve Regina University

When Travel Channel came to Newport in the summer of 2002 to work on a ghost feature, Salve Regina was asked to look into its ghostly history, something the institution had previously paid little heed to.

One of the most interesting tales it discovered was that of the White Lady of the William Watts Sherman House.

Salve Regina was granted a charter by the State of Rhode Island in 1934, but it wasn't until 1947, when the college acquired the Ochre Court, one of Newport's famed mansions, that the Catholic college was able to open. Its first class was fifty-eight students.

Ochre Court, with its breathtaking backdrop of the Atlantic Ocean, had been designed by prominent resort architect Richard Morris Hunt and was constructed in 1888-91 as a summer home for banker and developer Ogden Goelet.

As the college grew, it filled its need for accommodations by acquiring mansions and large homes in the neighborhood surrounding Ochre Court. The William Watts Sherman House, a summer villa, was designed by Henry Hobson Richardson and constructed in 1874-5, on property given to Sherman's first wife, Annie Wetmore, by her father. Sherman was a financier in New York.

The Sherman house was acquired by the university in 1982 and was listed on the National Register for Historic Places as part of the Bellevue Avenue Historic District, in 1972. In its function as a residence hall, it is home to 84 freshman students. It also is home to the White Lady and her son.

Sherman, who also was married to Sophia Augusta Brown, fathered several daughters, but no sons, so little is known of the relationship between the little boy and the Sherman family. What is known is that he died tragically.

"The son was playing with a ball on the second floor when it bounced down the stairs," says Kristine Hendrickson, director of media relations for the university. "He went after it, fell down the staircase and died. His mother was so upset that she killed herself in the house as well."

The little boy remains playful and apparently pesky at times and the sound of his bouncing ball near the second-floor staircase is unexplainable, but undeniable. The White Lady remains a formidable presence, too.

"She haunts the girls' floors, but supposedly acts as a house mother," Hendrickson says. "Whoever the White Lady is, she is very nurturing and protective."

South Carolina

Bob Jones University

Rodeheaver Auditorium sits at the center of campus at Bob Jones University

When most people think of colleges in Greenville, it's usually Furman University that comes to mind, but Bob Jones University, a conservative Christian school, is very much a presence in town as well.

Nearly at the center of its expansive, neat-as-a-pin campus, is Rodeheaver Auditorium, an impressive building of blonde brick surrounded by lovely landscaping. People have reported the sound of organ music coming from the auditorium even when its doors are locked and the house lights are all out.

An elderly man reading in a room off the Mack Library's main hall is one of several apparitions that have been reported. Another is that of a young girl in a long dress seen strolling through the Art Gallery.

Anderson College

Anna White, daughter of Anderson College president John E. White, still makes an occasional appearance in the Sullivan House, which served as the president's residence up until 1960. Several conflicting tales chronicle Anna's death but she makes her presence known by slamming doors, rearranging desktops and even playing a little air piano.

Wofford College

The century-and-a-half-old Leonard Auditorium, site of chapel services and cultural performances of all types, is filled with portraits of the college's presidents. But one disembodied pair of eyes seems to keep watch over all in the building. The eyes appear high on the building's east wall.

South Dakota

Dakota Wesleyan University

Century Memorial Hall was the first building constructed on the university's campus, in 1903, serving originally as a women's dormitory. In 1910 it was renamed Graham Hall after one of the college's presidents. A four-story brick building, it provided many of the comforts of home for its residents, including fireplaces, a parlor and a family-style dining room in the basement. When Dayton Hall was completed in 1956, the hall became a men's dormitory, and that's when Nelson arrived. A fire broke out in the hall and he jumped, in terror, to his death. He is said to make occasional appearances in the dorm ever since.

Tennessee

East Tennessee State University

The fussy spirit of East Tennessee State University's founding president, Sidney Gilbreath, still watches over the building bearing his name.

ETSU offers a world-famous graduate program in storytelling, and the school's ghostly tradition gives the students in the program plenty to talk about.

Gilbreath Hall is named to honor the school's founding president, Sidney Gordon Gilbreath. Gilbreath was education's boy wonder of the era. He began teaching in public schools before completing his studies from Hiwassee College in Madisonville, Tennessee. He graduated from college in 1890 and the next year was elected superintendent of public education for Monroe County, Tenn. He was re-elected two years later. In 1895 at age twenty-six, he became the youngest man appointed superintendent of schools for Tennessee. He held the position for two years and left to become president of Hiwassee College.

Sticking to what seemed to be a two-year-per-career plan, he left Hiwassee to open a law practice. Two more years later, he became a professor of school administration at George Peabody College.

After a stint as superintendent of Chattanooga's schools, he arrived in Johnson City to become the founding president of the East Tennessee State Normal School, where remained from 1910 to 1925, his longest stint. He used the position to build a great teaching institution and push for improvements in public education and designed the curriculum for all the state's normal schools.

Gilbreath was a leader and an innovator, but he also was a bit of a prig and his passion for orderliness often took on an obsessive tone. Even today, he's fond of closing open windows and doors, particularly in the building that bears his name, the university's original administration building. He's known to walk the halls, and some have seen his silhouette in the windows at night. No poltergeist effects have been noted there, but from a buttoned-down guy as Sidney Gilbreath, none would be expected.

The building was renovated in 1975 and now hosts the College of Arts and Sciences and the departments of theater, computer science, mathematics and the Bud Frank Theatre, but to Gilbreath, it will always be home.

Christine Burleson came to Johnson City at age twelve, when her father accepted a teaching position on the original faculty of the East Tennessee State Normal School. The campus essentially served as her playground. She graduated from Normal High School in 1917, followed by a string of degrees and certificates from colleges throughout the world: University of Tennessee, Vassar College, Columbia University, Oxford University and the University of Siena (Italy). She taught at several colleges, but for her, all roads seemed to lead back to Johnson City. She had taught briefly there in the mid-twenties, but returned in 1946 and taught there until her retirement in 1967, when she received the university's first Distinguished Faculty Member Award. She committed suicide in November 1967.

Burleson's scholarly reputation earned her a spot in the university's Women of Appalachia collection, to dispel the Mammy Yoakum stereotype of women from that region.

Burleson has made appearances in a variety of subtle ways in the hall that bears her name, but it's the eyes of her father in a picture upstairs that gives visitors the creeps. They swear the eyes follow them as they move in the building.

Other ghostly spots on campus include:

• Cooper Hall, home of a screaming ghost.

• Mathes Hall, which has unexplained cold spots and the sound of footsteps that follow visitors through the hall.

• Yoakley Hall, where the spirit of a young woman who jumped from the third floor is said to reside.

University of Tennessee at Chattanooga

Patten Chapel, Hooper Hall and Metro are said to be haunted, as was a mathematics building that was razed not long ago.

University of Tennessee at Knoxville

The James D. Hoskins Library is no longer the university's main library, but for many years has been a place where people went to sate their appetite for information. The venerable old building, which opened in the early 1930s, went a bit further occasionally, when the scents of supper cooking wafted through the stacks. The kind but shy ghost also was said to be fond of riding the elevators at night.

Folks wondered if the ghost would move to the newer Hodges Library, but the Hoskins Library, named after a fifty-year employee who went from faculty member to president, became home to the university's special collections library and the university's archives…a perfect home for a historical apparition.

Texas

Baylor University

Internet ghost sites are rife with the story of Elizabeth Barrett Browning haunting Baylor's library. The story of the frail poet's ghost appearing on the library's staircase holding a lighted taper is both dramatic and romantic. Library director Dr. Mairi Rennie has a word for it – "fanciful." She has another word for it, too: False.

Ghost Hunting 101 teaches that spirits tend to remain at places that are meaningful to them, and the Armstrong Barrett library, built in 1948, holds no significance to Robert or Elizabeth Browning. Elizabeth, who died at age fifty-five was buried in Florence, Italy. She and her family moved there in part to provide a suitable climate for her, who suffered from poor health much of her life.

The Brownings "never even visited the USA, though they would have liked to very much," Dr. Rennie says.

One other misconception is that the lovely bronze statue by Waldene Tauch outside the library building is Elizabeth. Not true, says Dr. Rennie. It is the character Pippa from Robert Browning's poem "Pippa Passes."

Our Lady of the Lake University

Even for students who grew up attending Catholic schools, nuns hold a special fascination. Perhaps it's the habits some still wear that give them their otherworldly allure. At the Providence Hall dormitory, for example, the spirit of a departed nun is said to linger there. At the Old Library Building, another departed nun who worked as a librarian still makes an appearance now and again by turning on the stack lights and occasionally toppling books onto the floor when the library is closed.

Texas A&M University

The ghost of Roy Simms, manager of the animal science laboratory, is said to sleep in the elevator of the Animal Industries building. Simms was working along in the lab one night, cutting meat. His knife slipped and he suffered a deep cut. Simms tried to climb the steps up from the basement, but bled to death before he reached the top of the stairs. To keep Simms from causing havoc by moving furniture and rearranging rooms, the elevators must be locked at basement level at night.

University of Texas at Brownsville and Texas Southmost College

The Arnulfo L. Oliveira Memorial Library has had a reputation for being haunted, but little evidence of it. Time and again, patrons have reported they felt as though they were being watched. In 2001, a group of ghosthunters visited the contemporary, two-story library and were able to capture on film an evanescent image of a male figure in a hallway. The image's identity has not been identified, but the library's namesake seems a good guess. Dr. Oliveira, a local boy made good, served as president of Pan American University Brownsville and Texas Southmost College before his death in 1980. The library was re-dedicated in his honor that year.

Utah

Utah State University

Everett took a role in a play at Utah State University's Caine Lyric Theatre and has never taken his final curtain call.

The Caine Lyric Theatre, home to the Old Lyric Repertory Company, is Everett's home.

"Everett is believed to be the ghost of an actor from a touring or road company that appeared at the theatre during its early days," said Patrick William, a senior writer in the university's Public Relations and Marketing department. "The theatre was built in 1913 by a prominent Logan family and opened as "the showcase of Northern Utah."

Today, Caine Lyric Theatre is used by the Theatre Arts Department at USU. During the year it is used for department productions and during the summer it is home to the Old Lyric Repertory Company, a performance company based in the department that brings in professionals from around the country to work with Utah State's advanced theatre students for a summer season of four plays.

Vosco Call, a former department head and founder of the Old Lyric Repertory Company, was instrumental in obtaining the Lyric Theatre for the university and for its original restoration in 1963. He also starred in the opening production of "Hamlet."

The Caine Lyric Theatre is owned by Utah State but it is not located on the university's campus. It is in downtown Logan.

"Our previous artistic director lived in the theater for a time and that is when Everett first manifested himself," said Colin Johnson, USU's Theatre Arts department head and the production artistic director for the Old Lyric Repertory Company.

Johnson said the company has a paragraph about Everett they distribute from time to time. It alerts patrons to a 1913 "Hamlet" playbill mounted on a wall there that was found during the 1960 restoration of the theater. Everett played the second gravedigger and received more laughs in his role than the first gravedigger. Everett did not appear for subsequent performances and the first gravedigger showed up with a brand new skull for his performance.

The stories get more embellished as the years go along, Johnson said.

As for Everett's antics, he lingers in the theater and makes his presence known from time to time. He has been known to stroll along the catwalks late at night, calling out to the technical crew and performers.

Sometimes Everett gets blamed for things that are not his doing.

"We have just completed a renovation of the theater and just prior to opening the theater, we heard a telephone keep ringing and everyone looked high and low for the cause of this telephone that rang at odd hours and we finally thought Everett had simply returned," Johnson recalled. "He tends to appear when he is bothered and we thought he had returned high-tech. It turns out it was a telephone in out new ADA chair lift."

Johnson said theater staff always tells curious patrons to keep an eye on the house's right rear loge. Not only does Everett have his own seat in the theater, he often makes his presence known by forcing the right rear chandelier to sway. Those in the know say he is simply expressing his displeasure at having been wronged by a lesser-skilled actor.

"There are people who swear when they have come in the back door and have gone across the stage, that they have seen someone sitting in the balcony on the right side, and when they proceed up through the house, through the foyer stairs there is no one there," Johnson said.

"There are many, many stories about someone silhouetted in the door in the back of the theater of the loge and all the doors are locked from the front," Johnson said.

Students tend to embrace the legend of Everett, he said. Johnson also said that in his three decades with the university, he has observed students relish the tales and love passing them on, keeping the legend fresh and alive.

"He seems to be disturbed," Johnson said. "He seems to like to sort of hang back and observe, but appears when the theater is occupied or comes in unexpectedly. He wants the theater to himself."

Perhaps one day he will be able to take his final bow and exit stage right.

University of Utah

A Civil War-era soldier has found the Special Collections section of the J. Willard Marriott Library to be the perfect spot for his eternal bivouac.

At first glance, Special Collections, on the fifth level of the spacious, modern library might not seem the most appropriate place to spend eternity, but upon further inspection, it seems absolutely perfect. It is there where the university houses its manuscript collection, a vast photographic archive, more than 40,000 rare books, maps and newspapers, and the university's Western Americana collection, which includes vertical and clipping files on ghost towns of the West.

Students, faculty and staff have reported several apparitions in the section. The old soldier has breathed down the necks of some librarygoers and has been seen disappearing into the stacks by others.

One startled visitor came face-to-face with the apparition, but noted the old soldier was visible only from the waist up. The specter lingered but a second after their eyes met, he spun around and vanished.

Other visitors have reported leaving the room empty and in perfect order only to return moments later to find the room is disarray.

Vermont

University of Vermont

When she named her South Prospect Street home Bittersweet, Margaret L.H. "Daisy" Smith completely understood the irony of the title. The Federal-style building had been built in 1809 as a store and passed through several owners until Smith, a widow, bought it in1928.

Smith's husband had died in a car crash in 1918, forcing her to strike out by herself in the world. When she bought the building, she decided to convert it to a tearoom on the ground floor and her home on the second level. She named it after the bittersweet (*Solanum dulcamara*) plants that grew in abundance at the home in Burlington they had shared together. Her husband had been particularly fond of the plant's brilliant purple flowers and red berries.

She closed the tearoom after a brief trial and opened a real estate agency in the building, naming it The Bittersweet Agency. She was successful in real estate and lived at the site until her death in 1961 at ninety-four.

Bittersweet House, on the National Register of Historic Places, now serves at the home to the university's environmental program. People who spend time in the building say Daisy has never really left. A gentle spirit, she is said to roam the halls in period attire. Her silhouette has been seen by passers-by through the windows at night. Lights come on in the wee hours of the night when no one's there and the building is locked.

Also at the university is Converse Hall, home to Henry, the spirit of an overworked, underappreciated medical student who couldn't take the long hours, hard work and the despair of the job. He hung himself, but still hangs around the building, turning lights on and off, closing and opening windows and generally letting everyone he's there and still cares.

Champlain College

A beautiful home with a distinctive tower dating back to 1888, Jensen Hall is now one of the hottest sites for campus lodging. Champlain College bought the building lock, stock and spirit in 1965.

The house is haunted by the spirit of a sea captain who once owned the home, but like many fiercely independent New Englanders, he keeps to himself and if he's still hanging around, he's certainly not telling anyone.

Virginia

The College of William and Mary

The Brafferton, one of William & Mary's oldest buildings, now serves as the college president's office.

In 1698, when the Virginia statehouse at Jamestown went up in flames, it provided an opportunity for Governor Francis Nicholson to move the colony's capital to Middle Plantation. Within the next year, Middle Plantation had been renamed Williamsburg and a grand plan for development was underway.

One of the young community's greatest assets was the College of William and Mary, which received its royal charter in 1693, the second institution of higher education in the colonies.

In the years since then, it has become one of the nation's most haunted colleges, and most students there maintain an appreciation of their ghostly forefathers and mothers.

"Most freshman halls go on a ghost tour through the college and Colonial Williamsburg that first year," said Sherry McDonald, a member of the

Class of 2000. "I did. That was the scariest night of my whole freshman year."

The Wren Building, the oldest academic building still in use in the United States, began construction in 1695 and was completed in 1699, but the ghost who resides there wears the uniform of a Civil War soldier and paces around upstairs, McDonald says. The college first served as a hospital and storage complex for the Confederate forces. Later it was claimed by Union forces who torched it in 1862.

Also on the part of the grounds known as the Ancient Campus near the Wren Building is the President's House.

The Wren Building, completed in 1699, is the oldest academic building still in use in the United States.

"They found some skeletal remains in the wall there," McDonald said. "The ghost there apparently likes to run up to you and give you a hug." Other visitors there have heard footsteps and banging on the upstairs floors.

Across the common from the President's House is a nearly identical building called The Brafferton, completed in 1723, which was donated to the college by scientist Robert Boyle after his death. College officials followed Boyle's wishes and used the home as a facility for educating Indian boys and teaching them English. Previously they had received instruction at the Wren Building and been housed in town. The Brafferton provided ample classroom space and accommodations, but for most of the boys, they could scarcely have been more miserable.

"The boys had to live at the house," McDonald said. "They weren't allowed to go outside, and if you saw one outside, you could shoot him."

Most of the boys had been taken away from their families and transported to the school against their wishes. Living there was hardly the enlightening experience that Boyle had envisioned for them. The conditions were spartan, the food was often unfamiliar, and the discipline imposed on them was often harsh. Living cooped up in the home was certainly depressing to the boys, too. They were used to roaming, running and playing free.

"The kids would break free at night and play in a sunken garden behind the Wren Building," McDonald said.

For some, just getting out into the fresh air and away from the house was enough to make them cry, and some still do. At night in that area, one can hear noises ranging from shrieks to moans. On clear evenings, many people have reported catching glimpses of young boys frolicking at or near The Brafferton, which now serves as the office of the college's president.

Other buildings of interest on campus include:

• Phi Beta Kappa Memorial Hall, named for the national collegiate honor society that was founded at William and Mary in 1776. Phi Beta Kappa Memorial Hall, named in the society's honor, is the college's performing arts complex and home to a ghostly music lover. Musicians and performers who stay late or arrive at the building early sometimes get a visit from her or hear her perform.

• Tucker Hall, used for English and literature classes, is home to a female ghost. "A female student committed suicide in a restroom there in the early 1980s," McDonald said. Students washing their hands or combing their hair have gotten a fleeting glimpse of her in the mirrors as she scurries off to class.

Montgomery Female College

The land on which the college formerly stood is now occupied by Christiansburg Middle School, but the tales of curious little Montgomery Female College still survive. Most of them surround the appearance and activities of three women: Virginia Wardlaw, Caroline Martin and Mary Snead, whose ghosts are said to haunt the middle school and cause strange moaning noises.

The school was founded about 1850 and conducted its classes in a local masonic temple until the building on the north side of Christiansburg was completed. The community was progressive and the college enjoyed an excellent reputation in its early years. Wardlaw became its principal in 1903 and was soon joined by the other two women. All were in their fifties, and all wore black dresses with veils. Their attire earned them the name "the black sisters."

Students reported they'd wake up at night to see the women standing watch over them. Once the student awakened, the women silently withdrew. Others saw them in graveyards, chanting.

John Snead, Mary Snead's adult son, came to the college to teach, but twice suffered serious injuries in questionable incidents, then died of burns after a mysterious fire in his bed. No one was charged in the incident.

His death and all the peripheral weirdness drove students away, and by 1909, the three women moved north. In 1909 in New Jersey, Caroline Martin's daughter Ocie was found dead in a bathtub. The three women were later indicted for her murder. Wardlaw starved herself to death awaiting trial. Martin was convicted of manslaughter and placed in a mental hospital. Snead was released and went to live with another son.

Randolph-Macon College

Washington and Franklin Hall, the oldest building still standing on campus, has had a small array of spirits pass through its corridors, resulting in the sighting of a few men who vanished on second glance. The oldest building, like many other old college buildings, was pressed into service as a hospital during the Civil War, which practically guaranteed haunted status.

Among the other haunted buildings on campus include:

• Mary Branch dormitory, where strange noises and mild poltergeist activity have been reported.

• Kappa Sigma fraternity, where footsteps are heard ascending and descending the staircase, even when there's no one on them. A blue mist was once observed in the private home next door.

• Thomas Branch dormitory and Pace Hall also are said to be haunted. Copley Hall was reportedly haunted, but has not reported any sightings in years.

Sweet Briar College

Colleges and universities react in different ways toward the ghost stories that have been attributed to them. Some practice denial. Others tolerate them. Many give the legends their due and place in the institution's history. A select few go further yet and embrace them for the uniqueness they bestow on their campuses.

None go quite as far as Sweet Briar, which devotes several pages on the college website to stories about the ghosts of the founding family. The site also provides a forum for students and alumnae to tell of their personal Sweet Briar encounters.

Most of the stories revolve around Indiana "Miss Indie" Fletcher Williams, who founded the college in memory of her only daughter Daisy who died in 1886 at age sixteen. The tales demonstrate the devotion Miss Indie had for her polite but playful daughter.

Most of the family members are buried on Monument Hill, which looks out over the campus, and as the title page of the ghosts section advises, "the founding family still watches over us."

Be sure and pay a visit to the site at http://ghosts.sbc.edu/.

Virginia Military Institute

Virginia suffered huge casualties in the Civil War and many of those soldiers had trained at VMI. The Battle of New Market was particularly calamitous, since Maj. Gen. John C. Breckinridge's 62nd Virginia Regiment was reinforced with 257 VMI cadets, most of them teenagers hastily sent the eighty miles north to New Market. Breckinridge held the cadets in reserve until their participation was crucial to the 62nd Regiment's success.

"May God forgive me for the order," Breckinridge said as he sent the young men in.

The cadets fought with grit and distinction and played a pivotal role in winning the battle, though at great cost.

When the fighting stopped and the smoke cleared, six of the VMI cadets lay dead on the battlefield. Three more died later of their injuries; one died of tetanus from a leg wound suffered in the battle. One of the young battlefield casualties was William H. McDowell, whose fictionalized saga became the subject of Elaine Marie Alphin's children's book, "The Ghost Cadet."

Even today, visitors to the institute say they see tears trickling down the face of the bronze statue of "Virginia Mourning Her Dead," by Sir Moses Ezekiel.

Benjamin West Clinedinst's 1914 mural of the same battle in Jackson Memorial Hall is said to occasionally come to life at night, with flashes of rifle and cannon fire and figures moving around on the painting.

University of Virginia

As one of America's oldest centers of higher education, it's apparent the University of Virginia harbors a love of books. The university also is home to the Rare Book School, which was founded in 1983 and found a permanent home at Virginia in 1992. The school offers a variety of courses each year for bibliophiles and professionals working with old and rare books.

Others on campus feel a special affinity with books, too. A pair of ghosts keep track of the operations of the university's Alderman Library. One makes students and others using the library late at night apprehensive. He treads the aisles softly, watches library-goers and sometimes they gain a fleeting glimpse of him.

The second apparition is a long-time patron, who has visited the library since it opened in 1938. He keeps the books in the Garnett Room neat and in perfect repair.

Another haunted site on this historic campus is Montebello, which had served as home for John Perry, one of the campus' builders. Students keep a wary eye on the lights appearing in the windows and listen for noises or conversations that originate within.

Washington

Seattle Central Community College

The old building's name is pretty sterile these days: Building 312, South Annex, but then again, it's not what it used to be.

Its history and heritage are much more interesting. SCCC's South Annex, on Capitol Hill near Broadway in Seattle, was founded in 1946 by Edwin and Elise Burnley as the Burnley School for Professional Art. The school had opened elsewhere in the city and moved to Capitol Hill later.

The founders sold the school in 1960 and that's about the time the strangeness began. There were the usual manifestations of a playful poltergeist: footsteps, appliances and lights turning themselves on and off seemingly at will. At an art school, where the students had so many items to master and mind, things were both humorous and frustrating. Students' pencils, pens, charcoal, Conte crayons and other items would vanish, then reappear. Items would fall off shelves. Pencils and pens would roll off perfectly flat tables.

But the Burnley poltergeist took matters a thing further, rearranging whole locked classrooms at night.

In 1982 the school became the Art Institute of Seattle and in 1985, relocated to Seattle's famed waterfront, leaving the curious old corner building empty, but not for long.

Seattle Central Community College, which began operations in 1966, acquired the Burnley building in its twentieth year, and the poltergeist activity has been on the wane ever since.

University of Washington

The Showboat Theater no longer exists, but in its heyday it was a barge transformed into a simulated Mississippi-style paddlewheel playhouse. Moored on Portage Bay, it was another nontraditional production venue for the university's drama department, headed by Glenn Hughes, an innovator and creative genius who had developed the Penthouse Theater, the first theater-in-the-round.

The Showboat's dressing room and backstage area were reportedly haunted, but little information remains about the apparition. The Showboat Theater was removed in 1997 and took its ghost with it.

West Virginia

Glenville State College

Called the Lighthouse on the Hill by the community it serves, Glenville State College was established in 1872 as a branch of the West Virginia Normal School, and concerned primarily with teacher preparation. Training the next generation of teachers has remained in the forefront of the college's work ever since. It became Glenville State Normal School in 1893 and Glenville State Teachers College in 1930. It received its current name in 1943.

But even a lighthouse has dark spots and though the ghost of Glenville has been around for more than eighty years, it has kept itself a mystery in many ways. Never seen and only heard, the spirit is believed to be that of Sarah Louisa Linn, who was bludgeoned to death at her home in 1919. Her murderer was never apprehended. The 66-year-old woman's home was located where Verona Mapel Hall, a dormitory named for one of the college's presidents, was later located. The dorm was torn down in the 60s or 70s, college personnel say.

The benign but occasionally noisy spirit seems to have made itself a home at Clark Hall nearby, where it wanders the halls, occasionally bumping into objects, but causing no damage.

Wisconsin

Marquette University

From its start in 1894, the Children's Hospital of Wisconsin has worked diligently to serve ill children, many of them poor, and many of them from other countries. As an independent, non-profit hospital, funds were often low, and the hospital was forced to move around, but the doors were always open to children who needed care.

The hospital's next-to-last stop is now Marquette's Humphrey Hall, an apartment building for upperclassmen. From the time the college acquired the six-story building in 1988 until the present, strange phenomena have been heard and observed there.

When students trying to study have complained to the apartment manager or campus security about the screaming of children nearby, investigation revealed no children in the area. A shy and elusive little girl has been seen hiding out on the fifth floor and near the reception desk. But call her name or chase after her and she disappears.

Other spirited campus locations include East Hall, a former YMCA that's haunted by Whispering Willie, an endearing little boy who drowned in the pool there. Today students at the recreation complex pool see him playing occasionally as they work out. A pale blue light that snakes through the hallway and chilling temperatures are manifestations of Johnston Hall, built over an Indian burial ground. A room in Mashuda Hall became the site of cold spots, unexplained incidents and poltergeist activity after a student committed suicide. After several weeks of eerie activity – and several scared-out-of-their-wits residents moved out – the room again is quiet and benign.

Ripon College

Raphael the Ghost leads the Who's Who of Apparitions at Ripon, a college whose ghostly history extends back to 1917.

One of the school's more contemporary ghost legends, Raphael made his first appearance after the college's Red Barn Theater burned in 1964. The theater department moved to temporary quarters in an old church on the edge of campus. Raphael first made himself known with his repertoire of eerie and spooky sounds, wails and noises coming from the old church's spire or basement. His bag of tricks grew to include disembodied footsteps, doors opening and shutting mysteriously and electrical problems.

After the theater department moved to new accommodations at the Rodman Center for the Arts, the ghostly hijinks continued. The electrical and lighting systems seemed to be the focus of Raphael's playfulness.

One theater major claimed to have actually seen Raphael. As the student took a seat in the empty theater and whiled away a few minutes waiting for her next class, she said she felt someone watching her. She turned around and faced what student Bev Christ called "an iridescent glow" in her 1996 term paper on the subject. After a moment, the glow dissipated.

In another tale, a tailback on the football team hobbled back to room 104 in Brockway Hall one evening.

A residence hall for junior and senior men, it was opened in 1958 and named after William Brockway, whom the college was named after until 1864.

The football player was not in the best of moods. He moved slowly and with effort because he'd injured his leg and it was in a heavy cast. Snow had begun to fall as he lay down and he fell asleep easily. A knock on the door woke him and he made his way to the door to find no one on the other side. He returned to bed and heard the knock again. Once more he got up and hobbled to the door and found again there was no one there. He closed the door but stood behind it, determined to catch the culprit on his or her next knock. The third knock came, a loud one at that, and the ballplayer, who had been watching the opening beneath the door for shadows, jerked it open, but again, saw no one there. He had seen no shadows under the door, either.

Among the other sites of interest on the campus are:

• Bartlett Hall, which was once a hotbed for ghostly activity, but since its renovation and refurbishing, it seems to have sent the ghosts on their way. When the building was used as a residence hall, residents used to complain about the voices and noises of furniture being rearranged coming from the top floor. Trouble was, no one lived on the top floor and it was usually locked shut. It was the hall's attic.

• In Scott Hall, a player on the college's football team was awakened from his sleep by the sound of someone calling his name. Upon awakening, he looked up to see a gray figure standing next to his bed, wearing his letter jacket.

• The college's oldest ghost tale takes place in Hughes House, where a handful of freshmen women heard wailing and looked up toward the upper-floor windows, where they saw a ghostly silhouette in the area the wails were coming from.

Wyoming

Northwest College

Some ghosts, like the colleges they inhabit, have humble beginnings. Northwest College opened its doors at the local public school in 1946. It had fewer than 100 students and was called the University of Wyoming Northwest Center. In 1953 it was renamed Northwest Community College and in 1989, it became Northwest College.

From its modest start, the college has grown and flourished. Its performing arts venue is the Nelson Performing Arts Center, named to honor R.A. Nelson, founder of the college's foundation.

The center is the home of a variety of performing arts for the area, but has occasionally been home to dramas played out by shadow actors. Persons inside the theater have seen the silhouettes of actors performing their roles, but the stage was empty and the lighting booth was, too. The theater also has some wicked cold spots, some poltergeist action, self-propelled rocking chairs, and a gentle female apparition who shows up from time to time.

Canada

Simon Fraser University

The mansion once known as Fairacres now serves as the Burnaby Art Gallery, and among its many uses, once served as a temporary dormitory while permanent facilities were under construction.

Throughout much of its history, it has been reputed as the home of a tranquil woman in white who moves through the walls of the building's third floor.

Construction on the mansion was concluded in 1909, about the time the clothing worn by another apparition, an elderly gentleman at the head of the main stairway, was fashionable.

Trent University

Scott House on the campus of Traill College is home to a caring female spirit who roams through the hall dressed in her nightie. She makes her first appearance of each year on the second floor, beginning in October. Her first sighting was about 1970 when the house was used for student housing. Her identity is not known, but staff members say she's friendly and caring and makes her rounds to be sure everyone inside is safe and well.

University of Regina

Francis Darke, who served as mayor of Regina from 1898-99, was also an entrepreneur, philanthropist, and supporter of the arts. He and his wife donated the Darke Memorial Chimes for Regina's Metropolitan Memorial Church in 1927. His support of what was formerly Regina College, where he has served as a member of the Board of Governors, was formally recognized with the dedication of Darke Hall in 1928 the performing arts center on the college's old campus on College Avenue. The building, with its 610-seat theater, was constructed across the street from Darke's home, which has since been transformed into a funeral chapel.

When Darke died at age seventy-seven, his body lay in state in the building bearing his name and his funeral was held there as well. Many say he's there still, watching the performers and enjoying the galleries. His presence – like his support, those who knew him say –is undeniable.

University of Toronto

The chapel at Trinity College is haunted by the ghost of a World War II-era aviator buried there, and the ghost of the college's founder is said to wander the college grounds.

A portrait of the founder, John Strachan, hangs in the Senior Common Room and spooked-out visitors there say the eyes follow them as they move about the room.

At UT's University College, the story of two rival suitors and the object of their affection is an enduring ghost tale.

A young woman was wooed by two masons working on the college's buildings in the mid-1880s. One was a Russian, Ivan Rezinkoff, the other was Greek, Paul Diablos. The woman eventually accepted Rezinkoff's proposal for marriage, but Diablos later told Rezinkoff that he had continued his courtship with the woman despite the engagement. Rezinkoff spied on the two of them and found Diablos' boasts had been truthful. Infuriated, he chased him with an axe, but did not catch him. Diablos escaped Rezinkoff's wrath, but ended the lovers' triangle himself, ambushing him and stabbing him to death. Diablos disposed of the body in a stairwell on the construction site. Rezinkoff's ghost is said to roam the campus still, looking possibly for the love of his life, or perhaps for his murderer.

Wanted: More ghosts

From Benoit to Olivet Colleges, Harvard, South Dakota State and Stanford to Ohio University, we've heard about the ghosts reputed to be hanging out in your dorms, theaters and classrooms, but doggone it, search though we did, we couldn't find enough about them to include them in this book. We're hoping you'll get in touch so your alma mater won't be left out in the next edition. What we'd like are your stories, plus newspaper clips, alumni magazine stories and other documentation.

Please send those stories to the authors at Schiffer Publishing at 4880 Lower Valley Road, Route 372, Atglen, Pa. 19310 or by email to cindythuma@yahoo.com.

Bibliography

Adams, Charles J. and David J. Seibold, *Ghost stories of the Lehigh Valley*, Reading, Pa.: Exeter House Books, 1993.

Anderson, Joy, "Grace ghost tales persist," *AquinOnline*, October 22, 1999.

Behrend, Jackie Eileen, *The Hauntings of Williamsburg, Yorktown and Jamestown*," Winston-Salem, N.C.: John F. Blair, 1998.

Boettcher, Graham, "Campus has many skeletons in closets," *Yale Daily News* (online edition), March 31, 1995.

Borowiak, Zachary, "Griesedieck Hall Haunted House Prepares to Scare and Share," *The University News*, October 28, 1999.

Breheny, Patrick, "Theatre de la Macabre," *Iowa State Daily* (online edition), October 25, 2000.

"Brown Lady makes annual visitation as usual," *The Chowanian*, November 8, 1923, pg. 3.

"Brown Lady is again a visitor at the college," *The Chowanian*, November 6, 1925, pg 1.

Burg, Kacy, "Legends at Wartburg," *The Wartburg Trumpet* (online edition), October 23, 2000.

Burns, Danny and Marjie Kosman, "Ghosts in the hall," *The Northwest Missourian* (online edition), October 26, 2000.

Burton, Rachel and Kristen Suiter, "The Presidential Ghost," *World Around You*, March/April 2001, pgs4-5.

Byers, Christine, "Students scour Illinois in search of Halloween thrills. But the most frightening area of Peoria may be right here on the ... Haunted Hilltop" *Bradley Scout* (online edition), October 27, 2000.

"By moonlight burned," *Life*, October 28, 1957, pg.97.

Byrd, Barbara Anne, "Brown lady visits new dorm," *The Chowanian*, November 1958.

Calef, Zach, "Football Phantoms," *Iowa State Daily* (online edition), October 24, 2000.

Calef, Zach, "Parlor Games," *Iowa State Daily* (online edition), October 26, 2000.

Calef, Zach, "Keep telling yourself...it's only a museum," *Iowa State Daily* (online edition), October 29, 2000.

Campbell, Allen, *Ghosts at Carlisle Barracks Army War College*, Columbus, Ga: Brentwood Christian Press, 2002.

Caughman, H. Shirah, "A light at the end of the tunnel," *The Hoya* (online edition), March 23, 1999.

Chaplin, Micah, "I see dead people…in Pierce Hall," *The Tack Online*, October 20, 2000.

Chestnut, Christy, "Maryville's Most Haunted," *The Northwest Missourian*, October 30, 1997.

Christ, Bev, "Folklore at Ripon College: School spirit? We've got 'em" unpublished student essay, April 1996.

Citro, Joseph A. *Green Mountain Ghosts, Ghouls & Unsolved Mysteries*, New York: Houghton Mifflin Co., 1994.

"Clippings," *The Manitou Messenger*, January 1887.

Crozier, William L., *Gathering a People: A History of the Diocese of Winona*. Winona, Minnesota: Diocese of Winona, 1989, pg. 283.

Curry, Pat, "Ghost tales: A few eerie stories of area hauntings," *Athens Daily News/ Athens Banner-Herald* (OnlineAthens edition), October 29, 1998.

Daugherty, Scott, "The ghosts, poltergeists, and demons next door," *The* (Baltimore County Community College) *Retriever* (online edition) October 30, 2001.

Dizon, Michael, "Ghost encounters of the scary kind," *Daily Illini* (online edition), Oct. 31, 1996.

Donahue, Ryan, "Behind the Masque," *Kansas State Collegian* (online edition), April 2, 2002.

Ewaskiewicz, Heidi, "Don't Look Now," *ECHO.UCA.EDU* (digital edition), April 19, 2000.

Fitzgerald, Brian, "Eugene O'Neill's ghost a permanent resident of Shelton Hall?" *B.U. Bridge*, October 29, 1999.

Fowler, Stan, "The Haunting of Brown Chapel," unpublished student essay, Lyon College, December 1985.

Gaede, Kendra Leslie, "Paranormal encounters on College Ave.," *The Carillon*, (online edition) October 29, 1998.

Gazdhyan, Nune, "The haunted houses of ULV," *Campus Times* (online edition), October 30, 1998.

"Ghosts are strangely absent on campus – or are they?" *OSU on Campus*, October 24, 1985.

Graham, Emily, "Cameras are a turn off for ghost at Coe," *Des Moines Register* (online edition), October 29, 2000.

Handy, John, "Ghost hunters sense a presence at UTB," *The Brownsville* (Texas) *Herald* (online edition), May 14, 2001

Hanson, Gloria, "Screes says goodbye," *Dakota Wesleyan Today*, Fall 2001, pg.6.

Hauck, Dennis William, *Haunted Places: The National Directory*, New York: Penguin Books, 2002.

Hendricks, Kelly, "A school searching for an identity," *The University Echo* (online edition), April 20, 2001.

Jameson, Laurie, "OSU buildings spooked by thievish poltergeists," *The Ohio State Lantern*, October 30, 1986.

Johnson, Amber, "Do you belong here?" *The Met* (online edition), Fall 1998.

Johnson, Sarah, "The Haunting/Ok, we're not in Amityville, but you'd be surprised how many places around are HAUNTED," *Arizona Daily Wildcat*, edition 10, 1992.

Jones, James Gay, *Appalachian Ghost Stories and Other Tales*, Parsons, W.Va.: Parsons Printing Co., 1975

Kennedy, Jessica, "Folklore and ghost stories on the University of Nebraska-Lincoln city campus: A compilation," unpublished student essay, January 1997.

Kennedy, Jessica, "Haunted Halls: NU campus is no stranger to the supernatural," *Good NUz*, Fall 2000.

Knupp, Karen, "Ghosts in Pem? True or Not, myths persist," *Eastern News*. October 15, 1976.

Lagrone, Riley, "Dead man on campus," *The Battalion* (online edition), October 28, 1998.

Lambert, Peter, "Believe it or not! A student historian punctures KSC legends," *Keene State Today*, Summer 2000.

Macken, Linda Lee, *Ghosts of the Garden State*. Forked River, N.J.: Black Cat Press, 2001.

Madden, Kevin, "Augie's Attic amazes again," *The Northern Iowan*, October 27, 1995, page 12.

McBride, Jana, "When the wind blows," *Iowa State Daily* (online edition), October 30, 2000.

McCarty, Christopher, "Red hat boy still stalks Thorson," *The Manitou Messenger*, October 31, 1977, pg.7.

McCoy, Janet, "AU's ghost 'Sydney' continues to haunt, AU students believe," Auburn University press release, October 26, 1998.

McHenry, Eric, "Theater imbued with spirit of founder," *B.U. Bridge* (online edition), October 8, 1999.

McKnight, Edgar and Oscar Creech, *A History of Chowan College*, Murfreesboro, N.C.: Chowan College, 1964.

Melber, Mary, "Kokosing and other ghost stories," (Kenyon College) *Alumni Bulletin*, Spring 1979, pgs. 4-5.

Melia, Janice, "The Duncan Files," *Kansas State Collegian* (online edition), March 1, 1995.

Mensch, Melanie, "UNL has its own ghost stories," *Daily Nebraskan* (online edition), October 27, 2000.

Mielke, Laura, "Ytt's ghosts," *The Manitou Messenger*, April 25, 1997.

Munn, Debra D., *Big Sky Ghosts*, Vol I.. Boulder, Colorado: Pruett Publishing Co., 1993.

Munn, Debra D., *Ghosts on the Range: Eerie True Tales of Wyoming*. Boulder, Colorado, Pruett Publishing Co., 1989.

Nesbitt, Mark, *Ghosts of Gettysburg: Spirits, apparitions and haunted places of the battlefield*. Gettysburg, Pennsylvania: Thomas Publications, 1991.

Ogden, Tom, *The Complete Idiot's Guide to Ghosts and Hauntings*. Indianapolis, Indiana: Alpha Books, 1999.

Olmert, Michael, and Suzanne E. Coffman, *Official Guide to Colonial Williamsburg*, Williamsburg, Va.: The Colonial Williamsburg Foundation, 1998.

Orton, Matthew, "Ghost stories," *Montevallo Today*, 81:4, October 1991.

Osorio, Alma, "Students say ghosts haunt the corridors of Zura Hall," *The Daily Aztec* (online edition), October 28, 1999.

Palmer, Debbie, "Those hallowed, haunted halls," *The Sun-News*, South Suburbs, (online edition), October 30, 1997.

Pilver, Mike. "I See Dead People." *FSView & Florida Flambeau*. February 26th, 2001: 13 & 17.

Price, Charles Edwin, *Haints, Witches and Boogers: Tales from Upper East Tennessee*. Winston-Salem, N.C.: John F. Blair, 1992.

Raterman, Nick, "'Tower of Terror' haunting some residents," *Argonaut* (online edition), October 13, 2000.

Renovations document, 22, Buildings Records, Box 106, Smith College Archives.

Rice, Sarah, "Alleged ghosts live on campus, haunt KSU," *Kansas State Collegian* (online edition), June 19, 2002.

Rich, Jason, *The Everything Ghost Book*. Avon, Massachusetts: Avon Media Corporation, 2001.

Robbins, Alexandra, "George W., Knight of Eulogia," *The Atlantic Monthly*, Digital Edition, May 2000.

Roberts, Nancy, *Georgia Ghosts*, Winston-Salem, N.C.: John F. Blair, 1997.

Rule, Leslie, *Coast to Coast Ghosts*, Kansas City: Andrews McMeel Publishing, 2001.

Russo, Robyn, "The demons that dwell in the district," *The Hoya* (online edition), October 27, 2000.

Rust, Max and Colleen Winters, "Witnesses say U buildings are haunted," *The Minnesota Daily Online*, October 31, 1997.

Scroggin, Samantha, "Haunted happenings in New Hampshire," *The New Hampshire* (online edition), October 29, 1999.

Secret passage story clip from *Smith College Weekly*, June 19, 1929, 22, Buildings Records, Box 105, Smith College Archives.

"Secret societies still thrive at Yale," *Yale Daily News* (online edition), August 3, 1999.

Severance, Tonya Toy, "Boo! Ghost stories of the Upstate," *Creative Loafing* Greenville/Spartanburg online edition, October 28, 2000.

Shaw, David L., "Wells: A place for women and a few ghosts," (Syracuse) *Post-Standard*, October 27, 1990.

Shaw, James G. Jr., "Union College ghost," *New York Folklore Quarterly*, 2:2, May 1946, pgs. 137-138.

Slodowicz, Andy, "Fabled ghost lurks around library," *The DePauw.com*, October 27, 1999.

Slovick, Matt, "William Peter Blatty: Author, screenwriter, director," *washingtonpost.com*.

Smart, James G., *Striving, The History of a Small Public Institution: Keene State College 1909-1984*, Canaan, New Hampshire: Phoenix Publishing, 1984.

Smith, Daryl, "Hunting for the haunted," *Arthur* (online edition) 33:1, November 24, 1998.

Spencer, Mark, "Ghost biker lives in MU legend," *Hamilton Journal-News*, Oct. 31, 1992, pg.2.

Stanley, Barbara, "Montevallo ghosts give spirit to campus," *The Alabamian*, October 20, 1988, pgs. 5, 8.

Stehn, Molly, "Augie takes a break," *The Northern Iowan*, October 30, 1998, page 9.

Strand, Megan, "Terrifying tales: Friday the 13th inspires ghost stories from university lore," *The Cavalier Daily* (online edition), April 13, 2001.

Stuart, Elizabeth, "Haunts around town fill thirst for mystery, fright," *The Maroon* (online edition), October 29, 1999.

"Students say woman in pink haunts Pomerene Hall," *The Ohio State Lantern*, October 26, 1990.

"Students wary of ghost as former Stockton Developmental Center," *CAPT Outreach* (online edition), January 2001.

Tan, James Kw, "Ghost legends continue," *The Alabamian*, October 25, 1984.

Tan, James Kw, "Halloween brings memories of ghosts," *The Alabamian*, October 30, 1986.

Taylor, L.B., Jr., *The Ghosts of Williamsburg ... and nearby environs*, Williamsburg, Va.: L.B. Taylor, Jr., 1983.

"The haunted campus: Ghostly stories from Aurora," *The Ithaca Journal*, Arts & Leisure section, October 25, 1990.

'The Haunting of Maricopa Hall," *Arizona Daily Wildcat*, January 26, 1995.

"The Legend of the Lady in Brown," *Chowanoka*, 1944.

Thomas, Ryan, "Ghost stories haunt theaters," *The BG News*, October 31, 2001.

Thompson, Kristen, "Book debunks myths behind secret societies," *The Yale Herald* (online edition), September 13, 2002.

Thompson, Rick, "Ghost stories," *Daily Utah Chronicle*, 104:32, October 27, 1994, pg. 3.

Tunnell, Bertram, "Nearly a century later, Stuart Pierson still haunts Kenyon," *Kenyon Collegian*, October 27, 1994, pg. 9.

Verde, Thomas A., *Maine Ghosts & Legends*. Camden, ME.: Down East Books, 1989.

"Virginia Halloween: historic ghostly apparitions," *The Digest* (online edition), Fall 1998.

Wagner, Mark, "Local legends of spooks, spirits," *The Northern Iowan*, October 30, 1998, page 9.

Warfield, Sarah A., "Green House is planning for the future," *Earlham Word online*, October 1998.

Wilson, Patty A., The Pennsylvania Ghost Guide, Vol I. Waterfall, Pa.: Piney Creek Press, 2000.

Woodyard, Chris, *Haunted Ohio*, Palo Alto, Calif.: Kestrel Publications, 1991.

Zahaczewsky, Theresa, "Spirits walk on UH campuses," *Ku Lama* (online edition), 2:11, October 27, 1995.

We also were fortunate to receive documents, clippings, books and other materials from the archives of the following colleges and universities: Chowan College, Murfreesboro, N.C.; East Tennessee State University, Johnson City, Tenn.; Kenyon College, Gambier, Ohio; Lyon College, Batesville, Ark.; Ripon College, Ripon, Wisc.; St. Olaf College, Northfield, Minn.; Smith College, Northampton, Mass; Stonehill College, Easton, Mass.; Southern Historical Collection, University of North Carolina, Chapel Hill, N.C.; Union College, Schenectady, N.Y.; University of Tennessee, Knoxville; Wells College, Aurora, New York

Index